Balancing Leadership & Personal Growth

Balancing Leadership
& Personal Growth

The School Administrator's Guide

Christa Metzger

Foreword by **Paul D. Houston**
Executive Director, AASA

CORWIN PRESS
A SAGE Publications Company
Thousand Oaks, California

For information:

Corwin Press
A Sage Publications Company
2455 Teller Road
Thousand Oaks, California 91320
www.corwinpress.com

Sage Publications Ltd.
1 Oliver's Yard
55 City Road
London EC1Y 1SP
United Kingdom

Sage Publications India Pvt. Ltd.
B-42, Panchsheel Enclave
Post Box 4109
New Delhi 110 017 India

Printed in the United States of America

Library of Congress Cataloging-in-Publication Data
Metzger, Christa.
Balancing leadership and personal growth: The school administrator's guide/
Christa Metzger.
    p. cm.
Includes bibliographical references and index.
ISBN 1-4129-2699-8 (cloth)—ISBN 1-4129-2700-5 (pbk.)
    1. Educational leadership—United States. 2. School administrators—Training of—United States. 3. Self-actualization (Psychology) I. Title.
LB2805.M47 2006
371.2'011—dc22   2005022991

This book is printed on acid-free paper.

06 07 08 09 10 9 8 7 6 5 4 3 2 1

Acquisitions Editor:	Elizabeth Brenkus
Editorial Assistant:	Desirée Enayati
Production Editor:	Beth A. Bernstein
Copy Editor:	Edward Meidenbauer
Typesetter:	C&M Digitals (P) Ltd.
Proofreader:	Jennifer Withers
Indexer:	Rick Hurd
Graphic Designer:	Scott Van Atta

Contents

List of Tables
and Figures

Foreword

A few months ago I was with a group of superintendents who were talking about their work and their lives. Having spent more than 30 years working as a superintendent myself or working for them in different capacities, I have a pretty good sense of the breed. One quality they share is a stoical restraint that tends to paper over their feelings and thoughts. They become very political when dealing with the outside world and emotionally closed when dealing with each other. There is a sense that vulnerability can lead to weakness and weakness spells doom.

It was in this context that I witnessed this particular discussion. So when one of the participants talked about what it feels like to go to sleep at night with your fist balled up under the pillow out of pain and the need to strike back, the words were raw and real. This acknowledgement of the pain and peril of leadership opened up the discussion and took it to a new and more honest level. It became clear that one of the first steps to resilience is to come clean about the pain you are feeling and to embrace it and release it.

During this same time frame I was sitting in the audience at the American Association of School Administrators National Conference on Education when one of our speakers, Dawna Markova, came on stage and announced that she had been thinking a lot about her superintendent audience and worrying a lot about them. She then asked a question that caused me to suck in my breath. She asked quite simply, "Who stands behind you?" She pointed out that as leaders they were expected to carry the load for their districts, bear the burdens of their staffs, and heal the needs of their children. They are asked to do this with inadequate resources and under sometimes hostile circumstances. So, in this context, who stands behind them?

The answer all too often is "no one."

School leadership bears a lot of similarities with other types of leaders. There is much to do and many responsibilities to perform, but the biggest difference is that school leaders have responsibility without authority. In education, accountability is centralized, but authority is dispersed. They are in the eye of an accountability hurricane without shelter. They are expected to offset the problems created by society with inadequate resources and invisible support. And they must do this in public. They stand alone, in the center of the area, without swords or sidekicks. It is this public "aloneness" that sets the role apart from virtually any other that I know.

I discovered this "aloneness" the first few days I became a superintendent. I had served for three years as an assistant superintendent in a large district. I thought I understood the job of the superintendent pretty well. I had worked alongside the superintendent, had attended the board meetings, and had been a trusted confidant. Yet, when I took over a small but high-powered school district, I thought I was prepared. I discovered that the distance between the chairs of the assistant and the superintendent was much greater than the few feet that had separated our chairs at the board meeting. My whole world and perspective shifted. I was the spot where the buck stopped and there was no one there to pass it on to or anyone with whom to confide my fears.

Although I had heard my boss talked about on the radio, written about in the newspaper, and excoriated in public at board meetings, I had no idea what that would feel like when it was me standing in the crosshairs. This has led me, over the years, to collect various metaphors to describe what it feels like to be that target. I have likened the role to that of a piñata. You stand there and people gather around you and hit you with sticks, hoping something good falls out—and the people with sticks are blindfolded. Another metaphor is that the superintendent of schools bears the same relationship to the community as a fire hydrant bears to a dog—and in some of the places I worked they were running in packs. One of the best metaphors actually came from a board president who suggested that my role was to be a "quick-healing dartboard." The most poignant came from Jonathan Kozol, who once suggested that cities needed school superintendents because they needed someone to die for their sins. It is no wonder then that superintendents and schools system leaders go to sleep with their fists balled up under their pillows.

In this context the search for the leader is a search for meaning. What would make it worth it? I have suggested that the answer lies in the mission itself: The question becomes whether the end is worth the price, and I believe it is. I have described the role as one of soul craft that creates value to those around it. It is true mission work because of what is at stake—the future of our country and the future of our children. Fire hydrants may serve as conveniences to the dogs, but they have a noble mission of protecting the community from harm. This is a noble and high calling. The destination justifies the journey.

But how does one survive the trip? That calls for marshalling your resources and creating a sense of balance in your life. This leads us to an assessment of what Christa Metzger calls the "inner state" of our being. We have to know ourselves, maintain an adequate supply of necessary resources—mental, physical, and spiritual. For leaders to care for others, they must first take care of themselves. And that is the point of the book you are about to read. It will give you tools for making the difficult daily journey of leadership.

When I was young there was a joke that went, "Sound mind, sound body; take your pick." Well, as the Greeks reminded us, there is no picking between the two. They are interdependent. And I would argue for a third element which is just as critical: a sound soul. The task for leaders in any realm, but particularly for school leaders, is to maintain a sense of balance among the mind, soul, and body and create methods of refreshing and replenishing the wellsprings for these three elements of our being. And the other balance that is critical is that between our professional and personal selves. An imbalance here is like trying to ride a bicycle with one flat tire—it is hard and slow going, and it will wear you out. And being worn out will not allow you to lead. The only way we can pull our fist from underneath the pillow is by creating a sense of health that involves all aspects of our lives. This book should help.

Paul D. Houston
Executive Director,
American Association
of School Administrators

Preface

Why Leaders Must
Take Care of Themselves

I wrote this book because I haven't always paid attention to taking care of myself. For many of my years as an administrator, I was a workaholic. I know that some of you reading this, if you are really honest with yourself, can identify with this. Are you so dedicated to your work that you sometimes forget to take time for those other, more personal, aspects of your life? When do you think about what you value besides your job?

I still work hard and have been called a "high achiever," but I have learned that the most important part of life is to pay attention to all areas of my life, to maintain a balance between my work and personal life, to be a whole person. I say "I have learned," but it is truly an ongoing process. Becoming aware of your need for a more balanced life, perhaps as the result of a personal life crisis, is the first step.

Gradually it becomes a way of living: to find time on a daily basis to do something for your physical, mental, emotional, and spiritual health; to discover who you really are as a person, beyond the job title and the professional role; and to know what you value most, your purposes in life, your mission for being here. And then, as this awareness becomes a part of you, and as you put into practice what this means, you begin to notice that you are better at your job, too. Others tell you that you are more patient, more reflective, sometimes less rational in decisions and more focused on matters of the heart. You begin to learn how to say "No" when a request doesn't contribute to the wholeness of your being. The stresses of the job don't get to you as much, because you react from the center of your being, and you have tools to respond more effectively in such situations. I have been working at this for many years and continue in my Personal Growth every day.

What I am describing in this book, putting into practice the strategies to help you become a more balanced person, is not easy. It requires constant awareness and the determination that you want to, and need to, make time for your personal life. But the rewards are great! They will open the gates, and give you the gift, to a richer and more meaningful life, both as a leader and a person.

LEADERS NEED A BALANCED LIFE

This book is based on observations, research, and experiences from my many years as a principal, a school district superintendent, and an educational administration professor. It is also based on my work with groups of administrators and on research I have been conducting during the past 10 years. I have observed leaders who reached the top of the ladder and failed, even with the best training in knowledge and skills of our profession. Their expertise and competence could not save them from the inner turmoil and confusion that resulted when they were attacked, maligned, demoted, or even lost their positions and careers. I am convinced that the leader's own inner state is the key to survival and success, to his or her personal and professional effectiveness.

A few years ago, a dear superintendent friend lost her job when a recently elected school board majority set out to get rid of her—even before they started their terms on the board. She was devastated and felt worthless as a person because her professional life had become who she was.

RESEARCH BASE FOR THIS BOOK

The experiences of my close friend compelled me to begin a study that would ultimately lead to this book. I sought out and interviewed 39 superintendents who had involuntarily lost their jobs (Metzger, 1997). Their struggles to find new meaning in their lives deeply touched my heart as I listened to their stories. Some of them had contemplated suicide or gone into a lengthy depression because their work had become everything that had meaning for them, and they felt that they were nothing without it. Their sense of self, their identity, was so connected with their work that they did not know who they were without their job.

Pulley (1997) calls the loss of a job one of the most devastating events a person can encounter. Some of the superintendents I interviewed were able to pick up the pieces; others had to face themselves first, find out who they were, and how they might rebuild their lives. These interviews made me curious about the differences among these colleagues, and I decided to continue my research.

In the fall of 2000, I conducted a national study (Metzger, 2003) of 128 urban school district superintendents and college of education deans to learn what strategies they used to cope with stress, relax, get away from it all, nurture their soul, replenish their spirit, find renewal, and keep a balance in their lives. I coined a term, *Self/Inner Development*, which I asked the participants in this study to help define. I also wanted to know what practices administrative leaders use most often for their Self/Inner Development and how they found time for such practices.

During the subsequent years, I continued my research and asked more administrators—this time mostly school principals at all levels—what practices they used and how they found time for themselves (Metzger, 2004). A total of 162 administrators responded to these surveys and interviews: 89 high school, middle, and elementary school principals; 21 beginning administrators; and 52 administrators from district levels and higher education.

Through my research, a definition of the term Self/Inner Development emerged as related to the following six themes: balance, self-actualization, values, personal improvement, inner focus, and relationships. These themes, as well as the strategies and practices used by administrators, form the basis of what will be discussed in this book.

A strong recommendation from these studies was that these themes and strategies should be incorporated into the everyday life of the school administrator as well as included in university administrator preparation programs and inservice professional development. I will address some ways this might be done in the last chapter.

SOME CLARIFICATION ON TERMINOLOGY

In this book I will use the term *Personal Growth* or *Personal Development* to describe the dimensions of Self/Inner Development from my studies. It is difficult, if not impossible, to find the right words to describe what I will call Personal Growth or Personal Development. Perhaps it would be helpful to describe it as distinct from the practice of Professional Development, something with which all administrators are quite familiar. Professional Development focuses on knowledge and skills required for the job. Personal Growth or Personal Development is more about the individual who holds that job.

I will use the term Personal Growth as essentially a process that involves the inner life of the leader/administrator as a person: your sense of self;

the essence, the soul, the heart of who you are; your personal identity; that subjective core that determines your life's purpose; that which is the seat of your core values; the ground of your being from which arise your actions and decisions. More specifically, Personal Growth (or Personal Development) describes the following:

- What you do to get to know yourself better: Your values, needs, dreams, life goals, motivation, deepest desires; paying attention to your inner life.
- How you can become a more whole person, so that you are able to recognize and fulfill your potential in all aspects of your being: Mental, emotional, physical, psychological, and spiritual.
- How you can improve yourself as a person: Living each moment of your life more fully, developing habits that foster your total well-being in your daily life.
- Being more aware of the need for a balanced life: Spending the right amount of time and energy on work as well as play, time alone as well as time with others, keeping a perspective on all of your activities and measuring their effectiveness in terms of the central meaning and purpose of your life.

It is not easy to find the right words for such dimensions of being. Throughout the ages, many terms have been used by psychologists, philosophers, theologians, and spiritual leaders to refer to this aspect of human existence. C. G. Jung (Jaffe, 1989) called it *individuation*. Goleman (1995) called it *emotional intelligence*. Frankl (1984) described it as man's search for meaning. Covey (2004) made it the 8th habit of highly successful people, requiring what he termed *spiritual intelligence*. Csikszentmihalyi (1996) related it to the experience of *flow*. Senge (1990) labeled it *the fifth discipline*. Walsh (1999) referred to this as "central practices to awaken heart and mind." Bolman and Deal (1995) portrayed it as "leading with soul." Michael Thompson (2000) used the term the *congruent life* and defined it as following the inward path to fulfilling work and inspired leadership, connecting what we do for personal fulfillment and what we do for a living.

THIS BOOK IS DEDICATED TO THESE REAL LEADERS

This book is dedicated it to all of my administrator friends and colleagues over the many years who symbolize the inner strength and the determination to keep going despite personal attacks and unexpected twists in their careers. I have changed their names, but they are real.

To Superintendent Bill, whose school board turned against him and didn't renew his contract. Bill had given many years to this district as a teacher and administrator. He became so disillusioned that he left education and is now working in construction. I imagine he will be working his way up to be job superintendent or project manager soon.

To Lisa, a dear principal colleague whose teachers got together a petition to convince the superintendent to get rid of her; it was something about her communication style. I don't know what she'd done wrong, and I don't think she did either. Luckily she found another principalship in a different district.

To Gary, whose school board asked him to fire one of the high school principals in the district. This principal had been popular with his community and, after his dismissal, ran for the school board. He convinced the other new board members to terminate Superintendent Gary. Because Gary was near the end of his career, he moved to another state and took a university teaching position.

To Mary, whose contract was bought out by her board when things began to snowball around a custodian, a neighbor of a newly elected board member, whom Mary had documented for dismissal because of his excessive absences. Mary took an assistant superintendency in another district.

And to the many other administrators who were mostly highly competent, well prepared, and good people who fell victim to something related not to their job skills, but to the political climate in which they found themselves. Many survived and moved on to other positions; some are still struggling to find new meaning for their lives.

I also dedicate this book to the many administrators who are bravely facing the daily stresses of their jobs, who are the quiet heroes and the champions of the schools and districts they serve.

FOR WHOM AND WHY THIS BOOK WAS WRITTEN

The content of this book will be useful to all types of administrators and educational leaders, including district level, county, or state, and higher education administrators, men and women administrators, beginning level and those close to retirement. Even those who are not administrators (yet) might benefit from reading this book.

What unites all of these positions is the very nature of the administrator's job. The stresses, the workload, the constant demands of others on the administrator's time, and the continuous criticisms when making decisions have created a need for more attention to the personal dimensions of the leader's life.

One commonly felt need among administrators is their desire to find a healthy balance between their personal and professional lives and the realization of how difficult this is to attain. According to Senge (1990), keeping a balance between personal and professional lives has become a dominant issue for leaders. Such a balance becomes especially critical in times of crisis, change, and disappointments such as loss of a job, demotion or transfer, or personal losses, such as divorce, ill health, or the death of a loved one.

The issues addressed in this book will not only support individual leaders, but I hope that this book will ultimately contribute to addressing the current shortage of administrators. The lack of qualified persons interested in becoming school principals and the frequent turnover of administrators, particularly in the superintendency, have been well documented. When administrators learn to take better care of themselves, I believe that there will be fewer who will leave the profession, and more who will want to become school leaders. There will be fewer who will suffer burnout, and more who will remain vibrant and effective in their jobs.

Most importantly, I know that this book will help you as a leader to be more successful at focusing on the most critical goal of all education professionals: to promote maximum student learning while staying healthy and balanced yourself. To reach the highest ideals of your chosen work as an educator, you must keep a balance in your own life and pay adequate attention to yourself, especially your inner self. You must make yourself a priority, as I read in an advertisement for a resort in Sedona. Peter Block (Block, 1993, p. 77) writes, "If there is no transformation inside each of us, all the structural change in the world will have no impact on our institutions."

This book is for you if any of these descriptions fit you. If you . . .

- love your job most of the time, but feel you are often too busy with your work responsibilities
- feel stressed by too many obligations
- feel that you don't have enough time to do everything you're expected to do
- are concerned that you're not taking enough time for yourself or for your family
- sometimes wonder why you're in this job and how it relates to the rest of your life goals
- have ever wondered when you're going to burn out if your pace and stress level continue as they have
- just want to learn a few more ways to be better at taking care of yourself

You may not be able to change the nature of your job, or control what life offers you, but you can change how you respond to it. You can learn to take care of yourself, so that you can be the kind of educational leader that you dreamed of being when you first wanted to become an administrator. You can rediscover how you can make a difference in the lives of the young people in our schools. The key to an effective organization is its leader. Leaders must be whole themselves in order to serve others.

HOW IS THIS BOOK UNIQUE?

This book is a kind of self-help book in that it hopes to inspire you, and give you suggestions for how to help yourself to be more balanced. But it goes beyond the affirmations and suggestions that are typical of such books.

First, this book is unique because it seeks to engage the reader in an open discussion of all dimensions related to Personal Growth. This includes some terms, such as spirituality and religion, which are often avoided in academic and professional circles. Throughout the book it has been my intent to be inclusive and sensitive to the fact that some readers will have a personal religious belief system and others will not. Readers who do not subscribe to any particular faith or religious conviction may still acknowledge the existence of a power greater than themselves, some invisible reality which they may call spiritual. Examples and quotes used represent various religions and philosophies. The exercises and practices in this book may be adapted to suit each individual's personal viewpoints. Even for a reader who may not accept higher levels of consciousness, these practices will still be good for you as a human being. For a discussion of these and other similar terms, check the section on terminology in chapter 2.

Second, these practices have the potential to affect a deeper place within you, a real transformation, because they engage you through actual experiences with practices that have been used and advocated by both Eastern and Western spiritual and religious traditions from ancient times.

Third, the practices I will describe are based on research done with practicing school administrators—educational leaders like you. Their experiences will be useful for you to discover how your colleagues are taking care of their Personal Growth. I have included stories about real school administrators to illustrate the concepts presented.

Finally, the practices included in this book are comprehensive and allow you choices depending on your own needs and interests. This book gives you access to a variety of strategies for your Personal Growth and Development. I have also incorporated references to other books for each particular practice so that you may read more in depth on a topic that interests you.

SCOPE AND ORGANIZATION OF THE BOOK

Chapter 1 addresses various aspects of the need for leaders to take care of themselves. What causes stress for administrators, and how stress and crises often lead us to reprioritize our values and pay more attention to ourselves, is a major theme of this chapter. You will meet Principal Steve, whose activities serve to illustrate why it is important for you to know yourself and maintain a balanced life. The documented current shortage of persons willing to take on the job of a school administrator may have something to do with this lack of balance. A short review of research about stress and burnout is presented, including how response to these affect your health and well-being. How a crisis in your life can create greater awareness of the need for meaning and for paying attention to your personal and inner dimensions is discussed, followed by a section on "Ordinary Mondays." This part illustrates that even boredom with the job, and settling into a predictable and unmotivated routine, signals the need for more attention to Personal Growth. The chapter ends with a reflection on the nature of the school administrator's job and highlights what it might be like to be a balanced leader.

Chapter 2 elaborates on the themes and definitions of Personal Growth and will introduce various dimensions associated with this term. This chapter tackles the difficult task of defining and describing the concepts for which I am using the term Personal Growth. As pointed out in the section on terminology above, this process involves subjective constructs, concepts that deserve discussion and need definition. I have defined Personal Growth as a process that involves inner dimensions of one's being that focus on these six themes: balance, self-actualization, personal improvement, values, inner focus, and relationships. This process includes words that administrators might not generally use in their day-to-day vocabulary, but that are unquestionably related to Personal Growth, such as heart, soul, spirit, religion, and spirituality. The chapter concludes with a discussion of what other writers have to say about such words and how these might be used in the workplace.

How to find time for yourself and for your Personal Growth is at the heart of success in balancing your leadership responsibilities and your Personal Growth. Chapter 3 provides some assistance with this by reviewing basic principles of time management and techniques for prioritizing time. The chapter includes specific suggestions from other administrators about how they have found time for Personal Growth activities.

What are these Personal Growth practices? Chapter 4 gives an overview of all of these and how they have been used by various groups of administrators. These practices are then described in more detail in the following chapters (5–10). Each chapter focuses on one of them, and provides motivation and recommendations for incorporating them into your Personal Growth: physical activities, reflective and recreational reading, creative work (music, art, writing), spending time for and by yourself (silence, solitude, meditation), dreamwork, and spending time with others. These chapters may be read in whatever order you choose, depending on what interests you the most.

The last chapter of the book summarizes how Personal Growth can be balanced with leadership responsibilities. It shows how and why such practices need to be incorporated in the preparation of school administrators as well as in professional development programs. The chapter concludes with a list of specific suggestions of how you can begin to do this as a leader in your school or organization. You will be invited to develop an action plan for your own Personal Growth that will result in your becoming a more balanced and fulfilled person, and a better leader for others. In the Resource notes for this chapter we will visit with Principal Steve again in "A Day in the Life of a Balanced Leader."

Every chapter concludes with a set of Reflections and Exercises from which you may select one or more to make the concepts in that chapter come alive for you in terms of your own practices. All of them have been tried and used by your colleagues in some way. You may adapt them to suit your own style and need. Most of the chapters also include Resource notes where you will find additional information and suggestions, including some graphs from my studies.

I hope you will make a commitment to one or more of the practices in this book. Choose something that fits your style, but also try some of those new to you. Take as much time as you need to develop these, but make them a habit and remain committed to them. Most importantly, don't become discouraged if you don't feel immediate results. It takes a while—maybe a lifetime. But I guarantee that you will find yourself on a wonderful and exciting journey to a profoundly richer and more meaningful life—both personally and professionally.

ACKNOWLEDGMENTS

This book began with the love for writing and literature instilled in me by my first teacher, Otto Strobel, in the German Volkschule in Leuzendorf. I am deeply grateful for his belief in me as a child. Since then, he has written many books himself, and we have become good friends.

I learned professional writing under the watchful eyes of my beloved late professor Howard Demeke. His memory will always be with me. I wish he could have known about this book.

It was Rachelle Benveniste who first inspired me to write from the heart in her magic writing workshops. To Rachelle and the members of my writing group I extend sincere thanks and appreciation.

When my younger sister, Ruth Wegner, wrote her book in German and I had it translated by my dear friend, Ron Adams, I became serious about publishing my own work. I was deeply moved by my sister's stories and by Ron's excitement in translating them, and am eternally grateful for their stimulation. From my sister I learned to find my own path.

The research on which much of this book is based could not have been completed without the grants from the California State University College of Education and the Office of Research and Sponsored Projects. I gratefully acknowledge the financial assistance provided by my university, as well as the encouragement to conduct this research provided by my colleagues in the Department of Educational Leadership and Policy Studies. The participation in the research, and the support of my Dean, Phil Rusche, was key for completing this book. In particular, I want to acknowledge the inspiration and reinforcement I have received from my colleagues Jeanne Adams, Audrey Clarke, Antonia Sims, Justine Su, Rick Castallo, and Bill DeLaTorre.

Special thanks go to my brilliant student, Kim Bowlin, for her assistance with data collection and analysis of the surveys.

For their expert assistance with the sections on art, music, writing, and physical exercise I acknowledge members of my Brentwood Presbyterian Church spirit group: Lois York, Sandra Beckwith, Alice Baklayan, and Bea Ammidown.

The constant support of my meditation group, in particular Michael Quick, Lynn Glenney, and Patricia Hughes, provided a fertile soil for nourishing the progress to complete this work.

The following readers did much of the initial review work on the first drafts of my manuscript. They kept me honest and offered valuable suggestions: Bob Cole, Elaine Gourley, Marisa Sarian, Ida Alba, and Alfredo Gamez. I am deeply grateful for their faith in this project and for keeping me in touch with reality.

Profound gratitude is expressed to Gordon Nelson for sharing his vast knowledge, insights, and wisdom, for guiding me on my journey into my own inner world, and especially for helping me to connect and balance that inner world with the reality of my professional activities.

To the dozens of administrators whose lives I have been privileged to share and whose stories appear in the book; their names have been changed, but their experiences form much of the backbone of this book.

Many friends over the years gave me the gift of their own creative spirit, and nourished my soul. Among these I especially acknowledge Betteanne Rutten and her profound poems and my soul mate Kathi Rippe, whose art is sitting and hanging everywhere in my home and office.

I am exceedingly grateful to my editor, Elizabeth Brenkus, for her guidance and her valuable editing and production assistance on the manuscript. I have especially appreciated her suggestions and patience with me on some of the terminology used in the book.

Finally, this book wouldn't have been finished without the patience, support, sacrifice, and unselfishness of my dear husband, Hank. His faith in me has sustained me in our 35 years together. His responses have been the touchstone to let me know if I was also practicing what I have written in this book.

Corwin Press gratefully acknowledges the contributions of the following reviewers:

Gail Houghton
Associate Professor
School of Education and
    Behavioral Studies
Azusa Pacific University
Azusa, CA

Kathy Malnar
Superintendent
Hudson Area Schools
Hudson, MI

Leonard Pellicer
Corwin Author
Dean College of Education
    and Organizational Leadership
University of La Verne
La Verne, CA

Dana Trevethan
Principal
Turlock High School
Turlock, CA

Joyce Uglow
Principal
Lyons Center School
Burlington, WI

Robert Vouga
Associate Professor
School of Education and
    Behavioral Studies
Azusa Pacific University
Azusa, CA

Robert W. Cole
Editor and Writer
Former Editor-in-Chief, *Phi Delta
    Kappan*
Former President, Educational
    Press Association of America
Louisville, KY

Marisa Sarian
Assistant Principal, Curriculum
    and Instruction
Pasadena High School
Pasadena, CA

John Kenneth Amato
Principal, Maple Place Middle
    School
Oceanport, NJ

Alfredo Gámez
Tolleson Elementary School Board
    Member
Tolleson, AZ

C. Michael Thompson
Leadership Development
    Consultant
Author, *The Congruent Life:*
    Following the Inward Path to
    Fullfilling Work and Inspired
    Leadership

Richard Castallo
Chair
Department of Educational
    Leadership and Policy Studies
California State University
    at Northridge
Northridge, CA

Anne K. Garceau
Principal
Hillsboro School
Hillsboro, OR

About the Author

 **Christa Metzger** is currently Professor in the Department of Educational Leadership and Policy Studies at California State University, Northridge (CSUN). She has taught graduate courses in educational administration in the master's and administrative credential programs at CSUN since 1995. She was recently awarded the Professor Emeritus status.

Christa has a doctorate (PhD) in educational administration from Arizona State University, a master's degree from the University of Florida, and a Bachelor of Science degree from Florida Southern College.

Christa has been a teacher and school administrator for more than 25 years in Germany, Arizona, and California. She was a school district superintendent for 10 years before coming to CSUN as a university professor.

Christa has been actively involved on many state and regional boards and has held leadership positions in community and professional organizations, including a term on the *Phi Delta Kappan* editorial board. In 1990, she was awarded the "All Arizona Superintendent" award by the Arizona School Administrators Association.

Christa has published numerous articles and conducted research in areas related to educational administration, in particular on how school leaders keep a balance between their personal and professional lives. She has made many presentations and conducted workshops for school administrators, university faculty, and others. She has led meditation in her church for more than 10 years. Recently she formed a group of artists, musicians, and writers who conduct workshops called *Creative Paths to Spirituality: Exploring Your Journey from the Head to the Heart*.

Christa lives part-time with her architect husband, Hank, on their 42-foot sailboat in Marina del Rey, California. They also have a home in North Carolina, where they plan to retire in a few years.

1 Taking Care of Yourself as Well as You Do Others

The trouble with the rat race is even if you win, you're still a rat.

—Lily Tomlin

KNOWING YOURSELF

The need to harmoniously connect our outer lives with our inner lives has been the subject of many books over literally thousands of years.

- Does my work reflect what I value?
- Do I know what I value?
- To what extent do the demands of others agree or conflict with who I want to be as a person?
- How do I maintain a balance between my personal and professional life?
- Am I paying attention to all aspects of my life?

These are difficult questions, but the answer may be found in the old adage *Know thyself.* If you work on getting to know who you are, not just in terms of what you do, but as a person with certain attributes, needs, and dispositions, as a family member, as a friend to others, you will answer such questions from a point of centeredness and purpose that unites what you do with who you are. Are you aware of your connections with the interior landscape of your life, with the invisible dimensions that include your mind, your emotions, your spirit, and the deepest desires of your heart?

When Principal Steve comes to school on Monday morning, his mind is on the parent conference he has scheduled for 7:30 to discuss why the eighth grade daughter didn't get selected to the cheerleading squad. As he approaches, he sees a fire truck in front of his school and is greeted by his agitated custodian because of a broken water pipe that has flooded the restrooms.

Steve needs to quickly sort out his priorities and be able to respond appropriately to each situation. Steve thrives on such challenges, but by the end of his 10-hour day, which will also include a bus accident, shortage of a substitute in the science class, a presenter who doesn't show up for the assembly, and the superintendent's call to get in that safety report that was due last week, Steve's head hurts and his mind is still racing on his way home.

He wonders if he did the right thing in each situation (he can't even remember all the ones he handled that day). What will he do about the fights on the playground that seem to be increasing? Why can't other people take more responsibility for tasks assigned to them, so that he doesn't have to keep checking? How will he find classrooms for the extra students he is expecting next spring?

In the evening, his family also wants some of his time, and Steve sinks into bed dead-tired at 11:00, not having had a minute to reflect on his own needs. He has had no downtime just for himself all day. He enjoys jogging, but hasn't been able to find time to do any lately. And tomorrow will be the same.

Principal Steve can take a few such days, but if he doesn't find some space to renew himself, it's only a matter of time before signs of stress will appear in his body and in his actions, and he will begin to wonder how long he can continue this way. This pattern of rushing from one thing to the next—is he doing any good for anyone, including himself?

The graduate students in my administration classes, most of whom are teachers, observe their own principals and wonder if they really want to go into administration. The apparent stresses, the workload, and the lack of time for their personal lives are barriers that loom large before those considering jobs as administrators. Administrators already in their positions, like Principal Steve, wonder if they wouldn't like to do something else—perhaps leave the profession or transfer to a small school in the countryside—before they burn out and become ineffective.

In today's working climate, the rewards of being an administrator seem to grow increasingly internal, as everyone seems poised to criticize and condemn the leader's performance. It's hard not to take such attacks personally. To survive, succeed, and continue to enjoy the job requires inner strength, courage, and the knowledge of one's purpose for being in such a position. It is no wonder that there is a shortage of administrators!

This chapter will look at some reasons why administrators need to live a more balanced life and pay attention to their Personal Growth. Too many administrators succumb to stress and burnout and can hardly wait to retire. Some become discouraged, ineffective, unhappy, and resort to a survival mentality while continuing in their jobs. Too few teachers want to go into administration because they see what their own principals have to endure. And everyone agrees that we need more good administrators and great leaders!

WHY IS THERE A SHORTAGE OF ADMINISTRATORS?

There is a well-documented shortage, a decreasing pool, of administrators, especially for superintendent and school principal positions (Cohn, 2001; Educational Research Service, 1998; Glass, Bjork, & Brunner, 2000; McAdams, 1998). Many states and universities have recently implemented a fast-track mode for preparing administrators to meet this need. I doubt if such rushed preparation programs will result in administrators who have the necessary knowledge and skills and the personal competencies required for the job today.

In her surveys of graduates of educational administration programs, Adams (1999) learned that one of the major reasons why so many students do not intend to go into an administrative position after they complete their preparation programs is that they do not wish to subject themselves to the workload, long hours, and stressful environment that they perceive to be part of the principal's job.

STRESS AND BURNOUT: THE CONSEQUENCES OF A LACK OF BALANCE

The following brief review of the topic of stress and our response to stress will be useful in coming to understand that one of the major reasons for paying attention to our Personal Growth is to better cope with the stress we experience related to our work and our personal lives.

A few years ago, the term *burnout* was coined when referring to teachers and administrators whose effectiveness went up in smoke, so to speak, because they were unable to take care of themselves while performing their jobs. Burnout is said to be brought on by unrelieved work stress and results in depleted energy reserves (Wax & Hales, 1990, p. 3).

Many books have been written on what causes stress, on various aspects of stress, results of excessive stress, preventing excessive stress, and managing stress (Benson, 1975; Giammatteo & Giammatteo, 1980; Miller, 1979). Early researchers in the field of stress, such as Walter B. Cannon and Hans Selye (Brantley, 2003), described the feelings you experience in your mind and body as a fight-or-flight stress response. In fact, Selye defined stress as a response to a stressor or demand.

In his classic book, Dr. Herbert Benson (1975, 2000) described the physical symptoms associated with stress and explored a multitude of practices from various religions, cultures, and traditions to recommend what he called the Relaxation Response. This technique requires a quiet environment, a mental device to calm the mind, a passive attitude, and a comfortable position for the body.

Since Benson first wrote his book, much continues to be discovered about the important connections between mind and body, between physical and psychological experience, and the impact of thoughts and emotions on health. I often think about what my friend Gordon, a Jungian analyst, said about stress in his lecture called "Gifts My Father Never Gave Me" (Nelson, November 14, 2003): "Stress leads to the birth of the soul, the birth of inner consciousness. You have to find your own soul—no one else can give it to you."

Many authors agree that stressful events, in and of themselves, do not produce stress. For example, King (1981) showed that the stress associated with certain events come from the individual's reaction to the event, and are based on the beliefs about the event or about the individual's relation to it, rather than by the nature of the event itself. Thus, it is our response to life situations that makes the difference in how we experience stress.

WHAT CAUSES YOU STRESS?

Awareness of what events seem to create stress for you is the first step to managing stress, and planning a different response. What factors cause stress for you?

Malnar (1996) summarized research on factors that contributed to the stress and burnout experienced by administrators, in particular of superintendents: increased workload demands, diminishing financial resources, lack of respect as professionals, lack of support, a sense of isolation, and powerlessness over decisions.

Here are some of the factors reported by administrators in my studies that created stress for them:

- work overload
- time constraints/workloads
- staff/personnel issues
- unrealistic expectations and requirements of others
- too many policies and laws
- political agendas of those in charge
- financial problems in the organization
- inadequate support from superiors
- dealing with parents
- inadequate resources and support

HOW DO YOU RESPOND TO STRESS?

If the experts are correct that it is our reaction to external events that creates stress, it supports a basic premise of this book that we need to take care of ourselves to effectively respond to the stress factors inherent in our jobs. Many experts emphasize that stress is experienced especially when you are required to make decisions in your job where there is a conflict with your belief system.

For example, Principal Steve really wants to get angry and tell the mother how unrealistic she is about her daughter's potential for cheerleading and that the tryouts were conducted in a totally fair manner. However, he also knows it might be best to control his emotions. When should he back down and when should he stand up for his beliefs? He knows he should finish the superintendent's report, but he wants to be at his son's open house that evening. The decision to choose one or the other creates stress which he perceives as having "too much on my plate."

You may experience stress if you have to discipline a teacher who has been your fishing buddy, or if you disagree with the new zero tolerance policy that requires you to expel a second grader for bringing a kitchen knife, or if you really believe that children learn to read in many different ways, but your district mandates a "phonics-only" program.

Knowing yourself, what you believe in a particular situation, what your ethical standards are, reflecting on the conflicts you are experiencing, and how to let go of some of the alternatives becomes key to managing stress. And knowing yourself has to do with paying attention to your inner dimensions.

STRESS AND YOUR HEALTH

The connection between stress and health has been well researched and documented. Studies have connected stress to a variety of physical ailments such as infectious diseases, heart attacks, ulcers, and even cancer. The consequences of stress overload include exhaustion, depression, estrangement from work, powerlessness, alienation, burnout, depersonalization, the meaninglessness of work, and premature death (Malnar, 1996). Goleman (1995) discusses research that linked toxic emotions such as anxiety (defined as "distress evoked by life's pressures") to onset of sickness and course of recovery.

Sounds scary, doesn't it? But we've all seen colleagues who've experienced it. You have perhaps felt some of these symptoms yourself. How do you respond to stress, and how good are you at taking care of yourself, physically, mentally, emotionally, and spiritually?

We also know that there is positive stress and that a certain amount of stress is good for you (Benson, 1975; King, 1981; Miller, 1979; Sweere, 2004). What leaders need is to develop effective strategies for coping with and managing stress.

The practices described in this book will help leaders to achieve a needed balance in their lives by getting to know, and taking care of, all aspects of themselves. By learning and selecting appropriate strategies, such as physical exercise or meditation, experiencing the power of creating something through art, or feeling the healing touch of a piece of music, the leader will gain a reservoir of resources to use in times of stress.

It is important to be able to recognize when stress gets too high. In the words of one administrator I interviewed,

> You can't keep doing everything. Take the pressure off yourself. You need time to reflect on the "tyranny of the shoulds" and which balls you can drop . . . Of all the balls you juggle, one will drop, and you'll get yelled at about it. Focus on the most strategic ones.

To this administrator, it was focusing on the people in his business. Ask yourself in each situation where your priorities are, which ball you can afford to drop, and to which request you can choose to say "No."

When I was a principal, I had a little card on my bulletin board right next to my desk that said "People before Paper." As a result of setting this priority for using my time, I tried to do my paperwork after most people had left.

Another principal friend of mine, Tom, had a habit of coming in to his office to catch up on paperwork every Saturday morning. I'm not necessarily advocating this, but it illustrated his priority to pay more attention to the human elements of his job during the week. By the way, Tom also took time to participate in a community softball team as a way to maintain his balance. Tom was always open to the needs of others, appeared relaxed, and was a great listener, because he took care of his own needs and knew what kept him going. And Tom was said to be the best principal in the district.

STAYING BALANCED IN CRISES

Another reason you need to take care of yourself is so that you will be better able to deal with the crises that are a part of the rhythm of everyday life. Personal or organizational crises can have a major role in creating awareness of the need for taking care of oneself.

Crises cause self-reflection and examination of the meaning of life. In their book *The Hero's Journey,* Brown and Moffett (1999) demonstrate that the quest for a new identity always leads through some crisis where innocence is lost, where some breakdown occurs, which then leads us through chaos in order to find a new way. Crises may be related to family or to the job. Crises make us realize how much in life is outside of our control, and we feel temporarily lost or frustrated.

The poet Dante is famous for his statement that "midway on our life's journey, I found myself in dark woods, the right road lost" (Pinskey, 1994, p. 3). Sometimes we feel lost, and what used to work for us no longer does. What are some crises that have impacted you? How have they led you to acknowledge your need for inner strength and perhaps a new identity?

Crises bring changes and send us into periods of transition. The psychological process people go through in such times includes having to let go of something, parts of their old reality. Discovering the new reality takes time, and the road there is often confusing and painful. Bridges (1991) calls managing these neutral zones one of the most difficult aspects of the transition process. In his chapter entitled "Taking Care of Yourself" he describes the inner chaos experienced in these neutral zones. One of his recommendations is to take time-outs for reflecting on what is happening and to experiment with new possibilities.

Think about when you have experienced a loss. Have you lost a loved one to death? Has an important relationship broken up, perhaps through a divorce? What about your physical health? What happened when you or a family member were affected by some life-changing illness? Have you ever lost a job? A serious reassessment of priorities occurs when such crises touch our lives. In such times one needs inner strength to cope, to survive, and to rise again, like the legendary phoenix bird from his ashes.

Even the everyday crises of the job can cause someone to lose his sense of balance and become one-sided. We have probably all seen an administrator who has given up and has chosen the path of least resistance, or one whose impatient responses indicate some unresolved internal conflict.

WHAT IS THE MEANING OF YOUR LIFE?

Stresses, crises, and changes in our lives cause us to examine the purpose and meaning of our existence. When we are young, we approach our careers and our lives with enthusiasm and courage, like warriors ready for battle, knowing we will win. As we experience some of life's disappointments and failures, we begin asking the important questions of life, and search for our reasons for living. When I interviewed the superintendents who had involuntarily lost their jobs, their situation forced them to ask such basic questions, and to examine parts of their lives that they had perhaps neglected in their busy careers.

How do you respond to questions about the purpose of your life? I have observed some who, as they age, become bitter, cynical, and closed off to life's possibilities. Others seem to be able to rebound and make new sense of their existence. Maybe you are too young in your career to even ask yourself those questions.

The "encounter with the meaning of life is the most important task we have to accomplish in the years after midlife," states Jaeger (1995, p. 16). Victor Frankl (1984), reporting on his amazing survival in a Nazi concentration camp, found meaning in little things to get him through the senselessness and despair of his situation. He developed a form of psychotherapy he called logotherapy (logo comes from the Greek word *logos*, having to do with "meaning"). What brings meaning to your life?

Each person discovers his own meaning by being connected with his inner self. By practicing ways of taking care of yourself and engaging in your Personal Growth, you will begin to find the answer to the all-important questions about your life's mission as a leader and as a person. It is crucial to know yourself and your purpose, so that you can stay on course through whatever challenges may come your way.

One of the administrators I interviewed said it this way:

You've got to reflect on who you are, the inner core of your Self. What are your values, your sources of strength? How do you translate who you are into your relations with others? How do you blend your values with the facts of your job?

ORDINARY MONDAYS

Sometimes it isn't a crisis that drives us inside ourselves and causes us to search for meaning. It could be boredom or weariness, fatigue, discouragement, or the tedious routine of the things we do. I call it *Ordinary Mondays*. It's that feeling of listlessness as you drive to work on a Monday morning, or when you have to do the laundry, when you have to sit in a dull meeting, when it's rained for too many days, or when you wish it would rain again. It is the time when you have to work hard at being a good listener as you hear the same parent complaint for the tenth time that week. It's the discouragement you feel when your staff has worked so hard, and yet your school's achievement test scores seem not to be going up enough.

How do you get through those dull or depressing times until you can feel light and energetic again? Here, too, you need some strategies to take care of yourself, some way of touching your inner core that gets you through this.

There wasn't much excitement left in my colleague Vic. He'd been a principal for more years than could be counted. He'd done and heard it all before—the same issues, the same talk at PTA meetings, the same reasons for why a teacher wanted that kid removed from her class. The faces were different, but it had all become boring and routine. Vic's way of dealing with this was mostly to laugh about it. He'd prescribe the same solutions and went home early every day. Somehow he got by and survived. I often wondered if he'd ever thought of self-renewal, or even knew that he needed it. But then he was just a couple of years from retirement.

Maybe in today's harsh reality of accountability, Vic too would have been more motivated to change. Not that he was a bad principal, but not much happened in his school. I wonder what might have ignited Vic's passion and sent a lively spark to those whose lives he affected. If I knew him today, I'd sit down with him and show him my list of Personal Development practices and perhaps have him find himself in one of them. But maybe he wouldn't want to listen to all that. I wonder what he's doing now in his retirement.

THE NATURE OF THE ADMINISTRATOR'S JOB

Greater expectations of our institutions by the public, the fast pace of technological changes, and higher stakes tied to accountability have impacted the job of the administrator today. This comment by a high school principal on one of my recent surveys illustrates how bad it may be getting: "If superiors would stop threatening to fire administrators, that would relieve some stress."

Administrators are caught in the middle of many conflicting demands. More work added, fewer positions due to budget cuts, longer reports to satisfy the doubts of those who perhaps don't even read them, and an ever-growing to-do list—these are certainly some of today's realities.

The impact of such a working climate on the administrator is clear. In such an environment, it is increasingly difficult to find time for oneself, for thoughtful reflection before making decisions, or for maintaining a healthy balance of all aspects of one's life. This has been called a loss of soul and the great malady of our century (Moore, 1992).

In *Leading With Soul,* Bolman and Deal (1995) ask the key question of whether the dazzling array of remote controls available to us today satisfies our hunger for a richer, fuller, more meaningful life, or whether our contemporary emphasis on progress has put us on a one-way street to personal anguish and social disarray (p. 5). They advocate infusing our organizations with soul and spirit.

In her study on the levels of balance between the personal and professional lives of women superintendents, Malnar (1996) described the phenomenon of work addiction. She found that many of these superintendents suffered from work addiction and seemed to be so driven by their compulsion to work that they demonstrated a profound loss of ability to control the level of balance in their lives (p. 114). Malnar also concluded that some organizations foster and even reward behaviors associated with work addiction because of their long-established patterns of excessive work schedules at the expense of personal time for oneself, family, or recreation (p. 123).

Do you know someone who is a workaholic? Perhaps you are one and in denial of it, as were many of the superintendents in Malnar's study.

In a recent journal published by the American Association of School Administrators (McKay, 2004), the subject of workaholism was labeled as a serious mental health problem for school administrators, resulting in negative impact on their families as well as on their productivity.

A LEADER WHO TAKES CARE OF HIM OR HERSELF

What does such a leader look like? In the last chapter of this book, I will further describe the qualities and characteristics of leaders who are engaged in their own Personal Growth. In summary and essence, such a leader is a life-long learner who pays attention to all aspects of her existence. She is a leader who seeks to maintain a balance in her life, incorporating all of her major life goals. Such a leader reflects continuously on his activities to make sure that what he does, thinks and feels, is related to what he values in life. A leader who is working on his Personal Development is not perfect, nor completely self-actualized, but seeks to get to know himself and what is important in his personal and professional life. He then allocates and prioritizes his time and energy toward those values.

How does this process work for such a leader? The practices described in this book serve as paths to one's inner self, helping the leader to get to know herself by touching a deeper part of herself and developing an awareness of all aspects of her being. When the leader makes such practices a part of her life, she will be able to live a more balanced life, a less compartmentalized life. She will be better able to handle the stresses and crises of her work and personal life. She will be better able to connect her values with her work—to relate "who I am" with "what I do."

In his best-selling book *Seven Habits of Highly Effective People*, Stephen Covey (1989) calls this Habit 7, the principle of balanced self-renewal. He includes four dimensions of renewal: physical, mental, social/emotional, and spiritual. He shows how this habit of balanced self renewal surrounds all the other habits, and is the one that makes all the others possible (p. 287).

By examining and transforming his own life, by engaging in practices for his own Personal Growth, a person will learn to be the kind of leader that all the leadership books in the world talk about: a servant leader, a transformative leader, a charismatic leader, a highly effective leader, a leader who will make a difference with her life and work. He is a leader who is able to lead with soul (Bolman & Deal, 1995). She is the kind of leader you and I long to be.

REFLECTIONS AND EXERCISES

Reflect on the following questions. You may want to record some of your answers in your journal and review them periodically.

1. Take a sheet of paper and draw a line down the center. On one side of the line, draw a picture or use symbols, to show what causes you stress. On the other side, depict what you do to take care of yourself when you feel stressed. Discuss it with a friend you trust.

2. Think about a significant crisis in your career or personal life. Write down the feelings and insights you experienced. How did this experience change priorities in your personal and professional life?

3. Which of your ordinary routines do you find meaningless? What could you do to change them?

4. What is your mission, your purpose in life, and how is that expressed in what you do in your job and in your personal life? List what is most important to you in the areas of your life listed below. Begin each category with "In my _____, I want to be . . ."

   physical health

   mental health

   feelings and emotions

   relationship with others

   spiritual life

5. Imagine your inner world as a garden. "By 'fixing up' your inner garden you can symbolically work out mental and emotional tensions relating to health and other situations in your life" (King, 1981, p. 116). Sit with this image and become aware of what is going on there. Maybe you want to draw a picture of what you see. Revisit your inner garden periodically and observe how it might have changed.

2 Defining Personal Growth

And all our knowledge is, ourselves to know.
—Edgar Allan Poe
(An Essay on Criticism IV: 396)

Dana is responsible for her school district's professional development. As she observes her group of administrators file into the room, she wonders how today's workshop will be received. Most of them are principals. Having just been a principal herself, she recognizes the stressful looks and body language of her audience. She knows that most would rather be back in their schools, and that they will have a hard time concentrating on the topic today and keeping from thinking about what they have to do when they get back.

Yes, professional development is important. Giving information about the latest laws and requirements is essential for administrators to stay on top of things. Dana mentally reviews the workshops she has planned for them this year: literacy, achievement gap analysis, state standards, testing, testing, and more testing, data analysis, qualities of effective teachers, emergency preparedness, performance-based evaluation, school safety, and several sessions on the No Child Left Behind Act requirements. Most will focus on providing necessary knowledge or improving the technical skills of the administrators. She empathizes with their already heavy workload and the stress they must be feeling. She reflects on what kind of professional development they might really need: maybe a stress management workshop, a time management workshop, or something that will help them more in a personal way to cope with the unending lists of obligations their jobs impose. But it always seems that the knowledge and skills parts of professional development are more urgent and thus take priority.

BALANCED PROFESSIONAL DEVELOPMENT

Do you remember that list of national or your own state's professional standards for educational administrators? There are three terms that are commonly used when discussing what is required of leaders: knowledge, skills, and dispositions. Now, be honest, on which of these have most of your professional development experiences focused? Probably the knowledge and skills parts! Have you ever heard much about the dispositions required of you?

According to Webster's *New World Dictionary*, the word *disposition* refers to prevailing aspects of one's nature; to traits manifested in one's behavior or thinking; to character, the sum of moral qualities associated with an individual; and to personality, the unique physical, mental, and emotional qualities of a person.

In my many years as an administrator, I recall having only one such professional development workshop that helped me to get to know and develop some dispositions. It was something on intuitive management. I remember that this experience had a major impact on my management style and behavior. With all the rational knowledge and skills training I'd received, I never knew that I could, and should, pay attention to what my intuition was telling me.

There have been some trends recently to add these neglected aspects of the leader's personal dispositions to the preparation and professional development of school administrators. For example, some universities have begun to include courses in their preparation programs that address the inner dimensions of the leader's responsibilities, having to do with values, ethics, and personal belief systems of leaders (Sergiovanni, 1992). Some of the professional administrators associations have been including conference sessions having to do with achieving a better balance between the personal and professional lives of leaders.

The work of Daniel Goleman (1995) on emotional intelligence is related to the concept of dispositions. Goleman defines emotional intelligence as the capacity for recognizing our own feelings and those of others, for motivating ourselves and for managing emotions well in ourselves and in our relationships. Bloom (2004) identifies emotional intelligence as an essential element of leadership. One of his recommendations for emotionally intelligent principals is "taking care of oneself." He explains that "it's no secret that school leaders fail not because they lack brains, determination, knowledge, and technical skills, but because of what is characterized as style or people skills . . . most preservice and inservice programs for school leaders ignore these issues" (p. 14).

DEFINING PERSONAL GROWTH AS AN INNER DEVELOPMENT PROCESS

The Personal Growth of leaders has too long been a sorely neglected topic in professional preparation and development programs. Some of the consequences of this disregard have been pointed out in the first chapter, resulting in health problems, burnout, and a shortage of administrators. I will use the term Personal Growth to mean a process of cultivating the inner and personal dimensions of being so as to gain a more balanced and meaningful life.

Many authors talk about the connection between one's inner life, one's center, and one's outer actions and decisions. Whitfield (1993), for example, emphasizes the importance of knowing one's inner life and defines this as including beliefs, thoughts, feelings, decisions, choices, experiences, wants, needs, intuitions, sensations, and unconscious experiences (e.g., dreams and fantasies).

Now let's discuss some of the terms and concepts involved that are associated with the Personal Growth process. The following six themes emerged from the definitions provided by the administrators in my national study (Metzger, 2003).

SIX THEMES OF PERSONAL GROWTH

1. *Balance:* balancing life and work, professional and personal life, and knowing how to prioritize and use time.

2. *Self-Actualization:* self-confidence, being happier, taking care of myself, nurturing my mind and self, authentic existence, internal measure of success, and becoming a fully functioning person.

3. *Personal Improvement:* growing, renewal, learning, and developing myself from within.

4. *Values:* clarity of personal beliefs, character, integrity, knowing and prioritizing my values, knowing who I am and what I can live with, being in tune with myself, and "to yourself be true."

5. *Inner Focus*: sense of inner peace, of heart, of being grounded, centered, and focused; spiritual peace; having meaning in life; looking at the whole person includes the inner person, not to let surface things outside drive major decisions; and living with soul.

6. *Relationships:* leadership inspired by personal vision; being reflective about my relationship to my work; energy; attending to my own needs as well as serving others; knowing how to take criticism without being hurt; freedom; and identifying what I can control and living within that.

HOW OTHERS HAVE DEFINED PERSONAL GROWTH

In reading about topics related to Personal Growth and Development in the literature of other disciplines, such as psychology and corporate business, I found that a number of authors have begun discussing the strong correlation between personal growth and finding meaning in one's work (Briskin, 1996; Conger, 1998; Covey, 1989; Mitroff & Denton 1999; Pulley, 1997; Walsh, 1999; Whyte, 1996).

In their study of corporations, Mitroff and Denton (1999) concluded that we are all on a spiritual quest for meaning and that the underlying cause of organizational dysfunctions, ineffectiveness, and all manner of human stress is the lack of a spiritual foundation in the workplace (p. xi).

A few educational writers have recently ventured into this realm because of an increasing awareness of the important relationship between organizational effectiveness and the leader's own inner state. Some books specifically written for teachers and administrators within the past decade have advocated incorporating themes of Personal Growth and matters of the soul, the heart, the spirit into the workplace and into the daily lives of educators (Bolman & Deal, 1995; Brown & Moffett, 1999; Jaworski, 1998; Miller, 2000; Patterson, 2000; Thompson, 2000).

Leading With Soul (Bolman & Deal, 1995) was one of the first such books. The authors state that

> . . . in the workplace, all of us need a language of moral discourse that permits discussions of ethical and spiritual issues, connecting them to images of leadership . . . Heart, hope, and faith, rooted in soul and spirit, are necessary for today's managers to become tomorrow's leaders, for today's sterile bureaucracies to become tomorrow's communities of meaning, and for our society to rediscover its ethical and spiritual center. (p. 2)

A courageous step was taken by the American Association of School Administrators (AASA) in a recent issue devoted entirely to spirituality in leadership. In introducing the nine essayists on the role of spirituality in school leadership, AASA's executive director, Paul Houston (2002), stated that "all leaders must be attuned to the third dimension beyond thinking and doing—to what it is to 'be' a human in touch with the divine" (p. 6). He differentiated between religion and spirituality: "Religion gives us a rubric for working with the deity, while spirituality is the energy that connects us to the deity" (p. 6). He called the work of school administrators "soul craft" and accentuates the spiritual nature of educators' work.

PERSONAL GROWTH IN THE WORKPLACE

One of the difficulties in discussing this topic is that the words and concepts used tend to be subjective and interpreted differently by various people. Another difficulty is that some of these terms are perceived to be forbidden and avoided in the workplace, because of their connection with what is considered the realm of personal or private opinions.

Some words, such as spirit or soul, are often used in association with religion, and thus approach the prohibition to mingle church (religion) and state (public schools). Most administrators tend to tread with great caution around this topic. Others avoid this topic because they perceive it to be associated too closely with the New Age movement and the touchy-feely part of certain practices that are not tolerated by the rational, reasoning, and strong administrative types.

Here are some words that are related to these more personal inner dimensions of the leader's life: values, ethics, heart, love, morals, spirit, meaning of life, soul, and spirituality.

Which of these words would you use in your workplace when talking to others in your organization? The use of such words would be one indicator of how open your work climate might be to promoting the Personal Growth of the people in your organization. In other words, if the people in your school or district feel free to use such words in their conversations, and if you as the leader promotes such open discussion, your organization may be more likely to be a place where people are encouraged to pursue their own Personal Growth.

SOME TERMS THAT DESERVE SPECIAL ATTENTION

Now let's take a closer look at how a few of the terms related to Personal Growth—words like spirituality and spirit, religion, and soul—have been defined and used by other writers.

Spirituality and Spirit

Mitroff and Denton (1999) in their national study of spirituality in corporate America found that there was nearly unanimous agreement on the definition of spirituality and on the importance it plays in people's lives. According to their respondents, "spirituality is the basic desire to find ultimate meaning and purpose in one's life and to live an integrated life" (p. xv).

The spiritual realm of our life is described by Whitfield (1993) as including our personal experiences and our relationship with our true self, our divine or higher self, and our higher power: "Ultimately, my happiness or fulfillment depends on knowing and living from and as who I really am—my True Self—and connecting that in a healthy way to my Higher Power and safe others" (p. 28).

"What is needed is a new understanding of spirituality and work that shows the natural connection between the two and connects both to the deep human longing for meaning and purpose," states Michael Thompson (2000, p. 7). He believes that spirituality is a much-misunderstood word and describes it as "the way in which people connect the activities of their daily lives with their wellsprings of deepest meaning" (p. 52). Spirituality is concerned with the relationship between the human spirit and the Universal Spirit (p. 55).

Spirituality is defined by Kundtz (2000) as "the meaning and values by which you live your life, combined with, for believers, the way you experience the divine. To him, the combination of God, meanings, and values is spirituality" (pp. 178–179).

The concept of spirituality can narrow our thinking, Kabat-Zinn (1994) believes, and prefers the word *mindfulness* to connote the same thing:

> . . . perhaps ultimately, spiritual simply means experiencing wholeness and interconnectedness directly, a seeing that individuality and the totality are interwoven . . . then everything becomes spiritual in its deepest sense . . . it is the inner experience which counts. (pp. 265–266)

Bolman and Deal (1995) believe that modern managers concentrate mostly on the rational side of enterprise, and that if they neglect the spiritual dimension, they overlook a powerful untapped source of energy and vitality. The main character in their story learned to summon spirit by embracing symbolic discourse of spirit: art, ritual, stories, music, and icons. They talk about soul and spirit as often being used interchangeably. Spirit to them is transcendent and all-embracing, the universal source, whereas soul is the personal and unique aspects grounded in personal experience. They believe that "to recapture spirit, we need to relearn how to lead with soul" (p. 6).

Spirituality is defined by Judith Orloff (2004) as a "viscerally experienced energy that opens the heart, enabling you to feel a higher power. You tap into love, an unlimited source of positive energy" (p. 50).

Steven Covey (1989) calls the spiritual dimension of leadership "your core, your center, your commitment to your value system . . . it draws upon the sources that inspire and uplift you and tie you to the timeless truths of all humanity" (p. 292).

Spirituality and Religion

The distinction between these two terms has previously been pointed out. Essentially, on our spiritual side as human beings, we are accountable to something or someone outside of ourselves. If you define that outside cause, idea, or person to whom you find yourself accountable, as a divine power (which you may call your "God"), then your spirituality would be linked to a specific religion. Spirituality and religion may be connected, and often are. However, in discussing the idea of spirituality, it is your personal choice how (or if) you unite these concepts. Here is what some other writers have said about this connection or distinction.

Respondents in Mitroff and Denton's (1999) study of corporations made a clear differentiation between religion and spirituality. They viewed religion as a highly inappropriate topic and form of expression in the workplace. Conversely, spirituality was viewed as highly appropriate. The authors' findings would certainly be true in the culture of our educational institutions as well:

> . . . lacking positive role models of how to practice spirituality in the workplace, many people—not all—are terribly afraid even to use the words spirituality and soul. Many of our respondents believed that more neutral words such as "values" which carry less emotional baggage, are more acceptable and less threatening. (p. xvi)

Religious differences have been the cause of much fighting and enmity in the history of humankind. Whatever your religion or convictions may be, however, you will probably be able to accept the concept of spirituality, that there is a spiritual dimension of each human life that deserves and needs attention. Whether you pray to a divine being, or just get in touch with your own higher self, you are addressing a dimension of spirituality, something beyond the rational and visible reality.

Each religion and spiritual tradition has its own theology and philosophy with numerous similarities as well as differences. There is no question that many values and qualities such as justice, compassion, and forgiveness are fundamental human qualities that are extolled by all major religions. Many believe that such qualities are strengthened with religion, but may also be practiced without a religious belief. In the words of the Dalai Lama, "the benefits that religion and spiritual values can bring and the contribution they can make to mankind depend on ourselves as individuals and whether we really put them into practice" (Walsh, 1999, p. x).

Soul and Spirit

Some writers use the terms soul and spirit synonymously. Those who differentiate use the term soul to describe something more personal. Bolman and Deal (1995) state that each term needs the other: "Leaders with soul bring spirit to organizations" (p. 10).

The connection between soul and spirit is emphasized by Kabat-Zinn (1994). He states that "no truly spiritual work could be lacking in soul, nor can any truly soulful work be devoid of spirit" (p. 269).

Roger Walsh (1999) uses the term soul simply to point to the deeper aspects of the mind and self (p. 65).

Other authors believe that it is difficult to define precisely what the soul is. Thomas Moore (1992) states that

> . . . this we know intuitively, that soul has to do with genuineness and depth . . . tradition teaches us that soul lies midway between understanding and unconsciousness, and that its instrument is neither the mind nor the body, but imagination . . . fulfilling work, rewarding relationships, personal power, and relief from symptoms are all gifts of the soul. (pp. xi–xiii)

REFLECTIONS AND EXERCISES

Here are some questions and exercises. You may want to record your answers in your journal and review them periodically.

1. What terms discussed in this chapter have a special meaning to you? Write your top three words or phrases and reflect on how these are important in your life. Become aware of how various people use these.

2. What does the phrase *spiritual dimension* mean to you personally? How have you applied this concept in your personal and professional life?

3. Which of the six dimensions of Personal Growth do you feel you are best exhibiting and living out in your personal and/or professional life? Think of an example. Discuss it with a trusted friend.

4. Set a goal for yourself in one or more of the six dimensions of Personal Growth described in this chapter. For example, "I will be more aware of maintaining an inner focus in my work."

5. Ask your department or school faculty and staff how they keep a balance in their lives. How do they pay attention to the Personal Growth dimensions of their lives?

In the Resource notes for this chapter, there is a page of "Words Used in the Workplace" that you may want to copy and carry with you on the job for a week or so. Keep track for a period of time of when you hear one of these words. Then review the words in this list in terms of how often you or others use them in your workplace.

Be a role model for using such words. For example, use the word "heart" sometimes when talking about people's feelings and needs—and watch the impact on those with whom you are speaking.

 # Finding Time for Yourself While Working on Behalf of Others

Nobody sees a flower, really—it's so small—we haven't time, and to see takes time . . .

—Georgia O'Keeffe

Time goes, you say? Ah, no! Alas, Time stays, we go.
—Henry Austin Dobson

THE HEART OF THE MATTER

So you agree that you want to, and you probably should . . .

- work less and play more
- spend more time on yourself
- spend more time with your family
- go home from work at a reasonable hour
- don't go into work on the weekends
- don't take work home with you
- stop waking up at night thinking about work

Acknowledging that you want to address such issues is the first step to doing them. Yes, I know, you've tried and feel that you've fallen far short of your intentions. You are not alone. "Overworking is common in organizational settings such as the public schools where there are competing and highly intensive demands" (Malnar, 1996, p. 123). Many administrators attend time-management workshops and leave with the best intentions, only to fall back into their former habits. Kundtz (2000, p. 6) uses the term *time famine* as an analogy for our situation today. He says that most of us spend our days staring at the huge "Mountain of Too Much" (p. 12).

So What's the Answer?

The answer lies within you. There is no magic bullet for how to find time for yourself and for those Personal Growth activities that we will discuss in the next chapters. But there are some approaches that you might find useful, as I have outlined below.

If you are interested, you might be aware of how some esoteric writers have discussed the perceived lack of time in our Western culture. From this perspective, the problem lies with our notion of time as a sequence, as a function of space and physicality (Versluis, 2004). By looking at time in a more circular fashion, connected with the realization that eternity is part of our time now, we might gain a different perspective on the whole issue of time. However, for our purposes here, let's stay with a more concrete and practical treatment of the subject.

My friend Lowell, a district administrator in a medium-sized school district, was definitely a workaholic. He truly believed that the district couldn't run without him—until he got sick. Not just the flu, but a serious heart attack that kept him away from the job for 3 months. I'll never forget what he told me after he came back.

"Everything went right on without me," he said sadly, but with a knowing smile. I tried to make him feel better, "But not as well as with you." But I knew by the way he looked at me that he had discovered something important. He knew that if he died today, somehow the world he had so carefully put together, his work world that he had planned and controlled, would go on without him. Someone else would influence what happened. Kids would still learn.

When you think long-term like that, you begin to realize that what you do is important, but not that important. Lowell found out that things went on just fine while he was recuperating from his heart attack. When he returned to work, I saw a difference in him. His desk wasn't always cleared off, he was less compulsive about getting things done, more willing to allow others their way, and he had to take care of himself—doctor's orders! Lowell learned to take time—unfortunately he learned this the hard way.

BASIC PRINCIPLES OF TIME MANAGEMENT

Years ago I attended a time-management workshop somewhere and copied down the following basic principles of time management. I don't recall their source, but believe that these are still useful today. I will use them as an outline for the rest of this chapter:

Time is life—it's all you have

Analyze how you spend your time

Set goals to get the most out of your time and life

Prioritize—you cannot do everything

One of the best little books I've run across, written years ago by time-management consultant Alan Lakein (1973), is entitled *How to Get Control of Your Time and Your Life*. The notion of time = life is the heart of all time-management practices.

Recent authors have emphasized the importance of living in the now (Tolle, 1999). Tolle talks about how our endless preoccupation with past and future keeps us from honoring and acknowledging the present moment. The past is a memory trace, stored in the mind, and the future is an imagined now, a projection of the mind (p. 41).

Do you sometimes live ahead of yourself in your head, and get tired just from thinking about the mountain of work you have to do today, the problems you have to solve, the commitments you have to fulfill? The time and energy you spend in such a mind activity robs you of the ability to just be present with yourself and others in this moment.

Perhaps in the early mornings, when you first wake up, work thoughts are already rushing into your awareness. Is that how you want to fill this moment of your time? You can't really do anything about these things right now. So, instead, focus on the morning tasks at hand; use this time to do something for yourself, and try to relax and enjoy whatever you're doing then. By resting your mind, you will gain a needed perspective and allow yourself the freedom to creatively meet the challenges ahead.

In one of my favorite books, *Wherever You Go There You Are*, Kabat-Zinn (1994) gives some simple recommendations for being more mindful of time and space. He suggests practicing waking up just a little earlier to take time and get in touch with your breath, feel the various sensations in your body, and mindfully touch those waking moments.

You have a choice to allow anxious thoughts to sap your energy, or you can let your thoughts pass by at times, and use such moments to refresh and renew yourself. I'm not saying that your mind shouldn't be intellectually active, of course. We need to use our minds to do what the mind does best, but we need to observe it, and make sure it doesn't control every moment of our time. Take some of that mind time and use it for being still, being present, enjoying just looking at the sky. Build in such moments for yourself throughout the day. Become more aware that how you spend your time is how you spend your life.

Analyze How You Spend Your Time

There are some charts available, or you can make your own, in which you may record what you do every half hour during a typical week. In fact I've included one for your use in the Resource notes for this chapter (Table R.2, Time Analysis Worksheet). If you have never done this, I would highly recommend it—yes, it takes some time to do this, but the payoff will be worth it. You may be surprised, or even shocked, at what you may find.

I did this once as a principal to help me be more aware of how much time I was spending in various areas of my responsibility. Needless to say, I found I was not spending as much time on my primary mission to improve instruction, because I was overwhelmed with doing routine management types of things. This activity caused me to make some significant changes in how I was spending my time.

Analyze which of your recorded activities might be time wasters that you could eliminate or reduce. For example, did you have to redo something because of lack of planning? Did you overcommit how much you could realistically accomplish in one day with the result that you were late to everything and had to rush through these activities, never mind the stress level this created inside you? Such overcommitments leave you no contingency times and no moments in between to catch your breath, to reflect, and to be prepared for unexpected events. Henry Kissinger is quoted as saying, "There can't be a crisis next week. My schedule is already full."

Maybe you could learn to say "No" more often, set priorities, and schedule more time for each event. Is paperwork a time waster for you? With the knowledge explosion and the amount of papers that come across our desks, it's no wonder we have to learn to speed-read and read more selectively. What about e-mails? How many do you get a day? How could you screen them? How much time do you spend responding? Respond you must, but become aware of how you could do this more quickly and effectively. Another time waster might be your lack of ability or desire to delegate, feeling that you could do it better yourself.

In the process of analyzing how you spend your time, you might discover that some things that take time could be done differently, or not at all. When I recently broke my ankle and couldn't walk very well because of a cast on my leg, I became aware of how many trips I was in the habit of making from one room to the other, carrying just one item. I realized that my compulsive need for order was causing a lot of time to be wasted. One administrator told me that he had absolutely done away with TV watching, except for selected programs that he arranged to tape in advance. How much time do you spend in meetings? Have you tried stand-up meetings and printed agendas to cut down unnecessary meeting time?

The point is that by analyzing how you spend your time, you might discover some ways to find more time—for yourself!

Set Goals to Get the Most Out of Your Time and Life

As an administrator, you are familiar with the processes of setting goals. You know that you need to first begin with a mission or vision. These are more or less philosophical statements that give direction and purpose to everything you do. These should reflect what is important overall, the basic or core values. Most administrators have been involved in creating one of these for their organization.

Have you done a mission statement for your life? What's important to you? What do you want to accomplish? How do you want to be, to live? What are your highest values? Your purpose for living? If you don't know, use the practices in this book to discover such answers, recognizing that they may change over time.

After you have your life mission statement, establish some goals that reveal how your basic values and beliefs will be expressed in practice. They begin to show how you can operationalize your values. Your organization probably has a set of goals, but do you have some for your own life?

Have you set goals for your personal growth? Goals in relation to your family, your role as spouse or parent? Goals for your relationship with others—personally and on the job? Long-term and short-term goals? Daily goals and weekly goals? Do you have a calendar in which you record your daily goals? Maybe you call it a to-do list. Check to see if this list includes aspects of your goals.

A list like Covey's Seven Habits (1989) could be formulated into goals for yourself. Most importantly for the purpose of this book, do you have goals for your own Personal Development? Take a look at chapter 4, where you will find an overview of the Personal Growth practices. Select at least one of them for your list of goals.

If you are really compulsive about goal setting, you will want to set objectives for each goal—and maybe even an action plan and timelines! But I'll leave those additional steps up to you. The important thing is that you have put something into writing that reflects what you will do in your various life roles in order to fulfill the mission and purpose for your personal and professional life.

Here is a caution about setting goals for your Personal Growth. Whatever you decide to do to make more time for yourself, it must be realistic so that it works for you. Yes, some self-discipline is necessary, but the motivation needs to come from within you by staying focused on your mission, your long-range purposes. There is a fine line between practicing something so that it becomes a habit and, on the other hand, forcing yourself to do something so rigidly that it becomes a punishment for you. As an example, when I first developed my habit of daily meditation, I set a timer and felt appropriately guilty when, on some mornings, I just didn't get to my formal meditation time. Now, if I know I just can't make time, perhaps because I only got four hours of sleep the night before, I set a goal to be more meditative in everything I do throughout the day. I also aim to include a formal meditation time at another time of that day, or make sure I don't skip more than a couple of days. It's the same, for example, with my physical exercise program. I couldn't imagine living without it, but have become more flexible in when I take time to do it. My body almost tells me when it's time. My mind knows I need to do it at least two to three times a week (an hour each). And so I make time for it. I don't scold myself as much when I miss, but it's become a habit for me. And so it is with whatever other Personal Growth activities you build into your life.

Prioritize—You Cannot Do Everything

Now comes the hard part. First, you have to become aware of how you're spending your time, and then set some goals for how you want to spend your time. Now you have to let some things go and make room for others.

A friend of mine was always complaining about not having enough time to do everything. Maybe you have a friend like that. She was a full-time housewife. Another friend, a former student of mine, is now an assistant principal. Let's call her Marta. She has two small children at home. I have never heard Marta complain, though she often expresses that it is not easy to make enough time for her sons in view of the requirements of her work. I know from her staff and her principal that she is a very effective assistant principal.

Somehow Marta is able to set priorities for how she spends her time. My first friend illustrates a principle of time management I heard once that "work expands to fill the time available for its completion." Please don't misunderstand me. I know housework can be a full-time job and I honor all my friend did to have a near-perfect house, home, and family.

The point is that we can always find something to do. We can always be busy. I heard a speaker once talk about the elderly lady who took all day to write a letter: First she took an hour to find her glasses, then to find the letter to which she wanted to reply, the key to the cabinet with her address book, and so on. The key question is, what are you busy doing? How do you prioritize what you do?

TECHNIQUES FOR PRIORITIZING

There are some techniques for prioritizing your time. I will discuss the following three as key to helping you sort out priorities: planning, communicating, and organizing.

Planning

Planning is a way to eliminate time wasters and focus on what's important. Do you . . .

- anticipate what might happen and plan for it?
- plan for possible waiting times—so that you're never just waiting but using such times for your priorities, one of which might be just sitting and reflecting?
- plan for times to relax?
- plan time in between activities for unexpected occurrences?
- use your calendar as a planning tool?

Communicating

Another way to prioritize has to do with communicating. Do you . . .

- assess your speaking habits to see if you speak too much? Perhaps you have a habit of over-answering or trying to immediately solve everyone's problems?
- listen well so that your response is targeted to address the real issues and to truly result in appropriate action?

- handle phone calls efficiently and effectively, or do you tend to chat on the phone?
- select wisely what you put into writing? Remember that writing a memo or letter takes more time, and it may not be as clear as face-to-face communication. Such personal communication may take more time initially, but maybe less time in the long run.
- conduct meetings to get things done efficiently, and yet provide adequate time for people to express their ideas?
- keep a calendar for scheduling appointments? Do you block out time for writing reports and other projects with due dates?
- have contingency and personal reflection time spaces between your other obligations, events, and appointments?
- have an open-door policy where anyone can come in and interrupt you at any time, or do you modify this popular practice by sometimes closing your door for some concentrated time, or to give someone (including yourself) your full attention? Other people are important, but so are you! Remember that you are the most important person in your life.

Organizing

Third, being organized is an important element in setting priorities.

- How do you prioritize the many letters, papers, reports, and requests for action that come across your desk? Do you have a system? Perhaps using an "A" folder for what is the most urgent and important, and writing a reminder into your calendar to begin a project a few days before it is due? Do you dare to throw away what you don't want to keep?
- When you have a long-range priority activity (such as a report to do), do you start a folder in which you can place notes of ideas or pertinent information so that when you get to the deadline, it will be easy to just put it all together?
- How do you manage your stack of things to read?
- How do you distinguish between what's urgent and what's important?
- Can you learn to leave some things undone altogether?
- If you tend to be a perfectionist, can you choose when it is not necessary to do such a perfect job?

If we understand that there never will be enough time to do everything we have to do, we will work on leaving some things undone and putting others that are more important in their place. I have learned to say, "I didn't take time for this," instead of "I didn't have time."

Essentially, all we have is time! How we choose to spend it is the challenge. In reprioritizing your time and life, remember to make some time for yourself, for your own Personal Growth.

TAKING TIME FOR PERSONAL GROWTH

Because the time element is so crucial in keeping a balance and engaging in activities for your Personal/Inner Growth, I have included specific suggestions from other administrators for finding time to do the specific Personal Growth activities that we will discuss in the subsequent chapters of this book (see chapter 4 for an overview of these). Everyone agreed that it is very difficult to find time, but that it must be made a priority. It has to be built into the daily schedule and made a routine part of each day or week. The following time segments were most often used by administrators to find time for themselves: in the mornings before work, on weekends, in the evenings or late at night, while commuting, or on trips.

In my surveys of school principals at elementary, middle, and high school levels, I included an additional category called "during the workday." Principals ranked the times of the week for their Personal Growth activities as follows (also see Figure R.1 in the Resource notes for this chapter):

- on the weekends
- end of the day
- mornings before work
- during the workday

The amount of time spent on Personal Growth activities during the workday for the 5-day workweek was less than half of the time that they spent on the weekend. The number of hours per week spent by administrators at all levels on Personal Growth activities is shown in Figure R.2 in the Resource notes for this chapter. The number of hours ranged from 2.88 hours a week (nearly 3 hours) for "Time with Family and Friends" to 0.09 (less than 10 minutes a week) for dreamwork. Here is the complete list (rounded off to the nearest quarter hour):

Time with family and friends: 3 hours

Music: 2 hours

Physical activity: 1 ½ hours

Diversions:	1 ¼ hours
Reading:	1 hour
Silence and solitude:	1 hour
Meditation:	½ hour
Creative work:	½ hour
Dreamwork:	¼ hour

The comments from administrators regarding how to find time reflected how difficult it was for them to find and make time for such activities during the workday. Below are some of the most frequently used phrases from the surveys and interviews of administrators about how to find time for Personal Growth activities. These may give you an idea for how and where you can make time in your life for your Personal Growth:

- make it a priority
- I almost always do two things at once
- these activities are integrated into my life, my soul, my heart
- just do it
- they are a natural part of my daily routine
- watching TV is a waste of time
- do what's important now
- it's a priority and my staff knows it
- delegate non-instructional work
- create a strong administrative team
- make a set schedule
- at the end of the day, it's me who matters, not the job, not others
- just make time
- plan self time
- stop at the gym before coming home
- make exercise and time for self as important as chores
- set a timer—spend a set amount of time, and then walk away from it
- get up earlier
- unplug the phone
- throw mail in trash (unopened if you know it's junk)
- be organized, so you don't spend your free time fixing problems
- try to keep your work at work
- if you don't re-create yourself, you will die
- schedule and commit
- set a limit on how long you'll work—when it's over, leave and forget it
- eliminate repetitive paperwork

- go directly home after work—do only essential chores when you get home
- create break activities to signal end of work
- dedicate Sunday to family only
- survival is dependent on knowing what really matters and what doesn't

REFLECTIONS AND EXERCISES

1. Write a narrative or a poem entitled "My Time Is My Life."

2. Write a mission statement for your personal and professional life. Can you combine the two?

3. Do a time analysis, as suggested in this chapter. There is a sample in the Resource notes for this chapter that you may use or adapt. Select a typical week. Develop one chart for your personal life (e.g., mornings, evenings, and weekends) and one for your professional life.

4. Complete this sentence: "I will give myself the gift of time today (or this week, or this month, or this year) by . . ."

5. Become aware of your moments in between the "have-to-do" activities. Fill them with something that pleases you: Walk to the window and look at the clouds, take a photo album off the shelf and browse in it a bit, water a plant, remove a dead leaf, brush your dog or cat, or just walk around the room you're in and stop to look around.

6. Look for places in your life where you can say, "That's enough"—and practice saying it.

7. Set a goal for what kind of a change you could make in each of the following time segments to create some time for your Personal Growth:

   before you go to work in the mornings

   during the day

   in the evenings

   on weekends

4 Strategies for Personal Growth: Becoming a More Balanced Person

Direct your eye right inward, and you'll find
A thousand regions in your mind
Yet undiscovered. Travel them and be
Expert in home-cosmography.

—Henry David Thoreau, *Walden*

STRATEGY OR PROCESS?

The word *strategy* is a good administrative word. Administrators are used to speaking in terms of plans, tactics, policies, approaches, and methods. I've used it here, even though I'm not sure that it is the best word to use when talking about becoming a balanced person. Finding a way to develop yourself from within, your own Personal Growth, is more of a continuing process than an achievement strategy. It might be considered similar to the concept of environmental scanning. When applied to your Personal Growth, it would involve getting to know yourself in terms of inner and outer factors, and then planning to address these in appropriate ways.

Other words one might use for this process of Personal Growth might be *path* or *way* because they imply a progression, a journey. Let's go back to Principal Steve. As Steve becomes aware that he needs to change something about his way of living, maybe because of a particular crisis, or when his family tells him he's becoming a real workaholic, Steve may at first use his head to rationally decide that he needs to do something about his situation. He may set some time during his day for reflecting and for thinking about how to approach this challenge of taking better care of himself.

This is a mental decision that requires him to decide on a strategy and is an important first step. However, the change Steve seeks involves another part of him, the personal dimensions, his inner self. There is no quick fix for such a transformation, and mental strategies alone are not enough. Our "hunger for wholeness" (Au & Cannon, 1995), our "search for meaning" (Jaeger, 1995) must involve something else that touches the heart.

PATHS TO ONE'S INNER SELF

What are some ways to achieve a balance and to take care of your inner self? There are countless answers suggested by spiritual and religious leaders, Eastern and Western philosophers, psychologists, self-help books, and well-meaning friends. Numerous writers have addressed the harmony and balance between inner and outer life. Many spiritual or religious practices have been advocated to address this topic. Depending on your own background and orientation, you have certainly come into contact with these and have surely tried a few. You can find lists of techniques in the self-help section of any bookstore. Many of these do have the potential to help you find and develop your true self.

The practices or strategies I chose to discuss in this book are based on what I found in the literature, as well as what other administrators said they did in answer to this question: How do you cope with stresses, relax, get away from it all, nurture your soul, replenish your spirit, find renewal, create balance in your life, and attend to your inner life?

PERSONAL GROWTH PRACTICES

Superintendents, deans of colleges, school principals, and other administrators who took part in my studies listed the activities below as activities they used for their Personal Development (Metzger, 2003).

Physical Activities: walking, running, biking, working out, exercising, gymnastics, jogging, gardening, walking on the treadmill, hiking, playing golf, yoga, skiing, swimming, horseback riding, dancing, weight lifting, tennis

Reading: biographies, fiction, recreational, some professional, car race magazines, news, books on tape, sacred texts, poems, politics, reflective readings; respondents read on weekends, vacations, and airplanes

Music: classical, jazz, folk; attending the symphony; listening to the radio (e.g., National Public Radio) while driving, as background music; playing a musical instrument, songwriting, or playing in musical groups

Silence and Solitude: sitting quietly, thinking, reflecting, smoking a pipe, driving a car in silence, walking the dog, jogging alone; enjoying the time before falling asleep or a few daily minutes to sit alone and take a breath; gazing at the mountains or at stars; building a constant relationship with God

Meditation: yoga, prayer, meditation while running, church, at symphony concerts, affirmations, chants

Dreamwork: Most of the comments made on this practice were related to reflecting on goals, not necessarily on dream analysis in the psychological sense of seeking insights for personal development from nightly dreams.

Creative Work: projects around the house, yard work, art (ceramics, painting, drawing, sculpture), crossword puzzles, photography, building dollhouses, Web design, scrapbooking, sewing

Writing: personal and family correspondence, e-mail, journals, reflections, letters to editors, articles, poems

Time With Family and Friends: travel, vacations, weekend trips, watching movies or television together, volunteer work, going to plays or concerts, recreation time, talking on the phone with long-distance friends, playing with grandchildren, visiting, playing cards; cooking, eating, drinking together; being with husband or wife

Other (diversions, hobbies, at home or leisure time activities): shopping, cultural events, historical places, art galleries, sporting events, movies, grocery shopping, gardening and yard work, browsing at bookstores, sailing, Internet surfing, taking days off, racing cars, bubble baths, massage, cooking, fixing things, cleaning, laundry, crosswords, watching television, filmmaking, playing bridge, home decorating, fishing, boating, home improvements, slot machines, riding motorbikes, flying, drinking a glass of wine, smoking a cigar, going to a vacation home, knitting, cross-stitching

ACTIVITIES USED MOST FREQUENTLY BY ADMINISTRATORS

Below are the comparisons in terms of which groups of administrators used the various activities, listed from those used most frequently to least frequently. The list for superintendents came from my 2003 study; the principal and beginning administrator data from the 2004 studies. You may also be interested in viewing the graphs (Figures R3–R7) for these in the back of the book under the Resource notes for this chapter; these will show the exact average ratings in terms of frequency used.

Superintendents

1. reading—reflective/recreational
2. physical activity
3. music (mostly listening)
4. meditation
5. dreamwork
6. silence and solitude
7. diversions
8. creative work
9. writing
10. other—time with family and friends

Beginning Administrators (see Figure R.3)

1. physical activity
2. time with family and friends
3. reading
4. silence and solitude
5. diversions

6. meditation

7. creative work

8. dreamwork

Elementary School Principals (see Figure R.4)

1. time with family and friends

2. physical activity

3. diversions

4. reading

5. silence and solitude

6. creative work

7. meditation

8. dreamwork

Middle School Principals (see Figure R.5)

1. diversions

2. time with family and friends

3. physical activity

4. reading

5. silence and solitude

6. creative work

7. meditation

8. dreamwork

High School Principals (see Figure R.6)

1. time with family and friends

2. reading

3. physical activity

4. diversions

5. silence and solitude

    6. creative work

    7. meditation

    8. dreamwork

All Principals Combined (see Figure R.7)

    1. time with family and friends

    2. diversions

    3. physical activity

    4. reading

    5. silence and solitude

    6. creative work

    7. meditation

    8. dreamwork

As the above lists indicate, the activities most frequently used include time with family and friends, physical activity, reading, and various diversions. The least used activities were times of silence and solitude, creative work, meditation, and dreamwork. It should be noted that I did not include "diversions" or "time with family and friends" as a separate category in my 2003 study. However, because these were listed so frequently by the respondents under the "other" category, I included them in the subsequent studies as separate categories.

An interesting comparison can be made between the finding of my studies and what is generally recommended in the literature in terms of activities used for Personal Growth. The activities not used very often by school administrators (namely creative work, meditation, times of silence and solitude, and dreamwork) are precisely those that are advocated most often in the spiritual literature as ways to renew oneself. I hope that this book will encourage administrators to explore a wide variety of ways to foster their own Personal Growth.

HOW DO THESE PRACTICES HELP WITH PERSONAL GROWTH?

All of these practices involve you in something you can do and in which you can become absorbed; thus they are practical and doable rather than complicated and theoretical. They allow choices for you that will match your interests and inclination. They are good for you in many ways—physically, emotionally, mentally, and spiritually. They have the potential to bring you in touch with parts of yourself that you don't commonly use when you are in that other mode of your life, your work.

They are effective, in part, because you have to take time for them. Your intent and motivation in doing them is a key to their impact on you. For example, engaging in a physical activity can be done with a competitive purpose, where you focus only on who wins or on how many miles you walked today. Or you can engage in a physical activity with an inner focus, allowing the body to strengthen and renew itself, listening to your body, breathing, and using your senses to be present with the activity. Spending time with others can be stressful unless you are aware of what is happening in the situation, of feelings, of what is important to you and to those with whom you spend time. Even creative work can result in more stress if your goal is to perform, to show off, to achieve something. What is essential is to give yourself completely to the activity with an inner awareness, to engage in it with the intent to relax, renew, and get to know yourself.

HOW ARE THESE ACTIVITIES CONNECTED TO INNER AND SPIRITUAL DIMENSIONS?

Physical Activities: Spiritual practices have traditionally included some form of physical expression, something related to the body. Religious observances may include kneeling; walking on a pilgrimage; bowing; even dancing, fasting, or eating well; and sitting still.

Reading: Reflective reading builds the soul, builds the spirit, and helps the mind to learn something in order to develop a new habit for better living.

Creative Work (Art, Music, Writing): All spiritual traditions include something to see, a visual image, religious art, contact with nature, or producing something beautiful. There is always something to hear, a sound made by a drum, religious music, a chant, singing, listening to bells, or becoming lost in the impact of a piece of music. By recording our ideas and feelings, writing helps us to get to know ourselves better and clarify thoughts and emotions. All creative activities assist us to get in touch with inner wisdom and provide an outlet for self-expression.

Silence and Solitude, Meditation: Every spiritual tradition and religion includes practicing times of silence, getting away alone, meditating, and praying to develop new insights and awareness for spiritual growth.

Dreamwork: Dreams, visions, and the imagination are often used to get in touch with something deeper and larger than our everyday existence. This could be our day dreams (our hopes and desires), or using the messages from our unconscious as revealed in our night dreams.

Time With Family and Friends: Relationships teach us about our own complexes and needs and how these impact others. We learn about the ways we communicate, how we behave in conflict situations, how well we listen, how we handle our emotions, and how we express caring and love.

Other (Diversions): Many of the items listed in the surveys in this category could fit into one or more of the other areas. Some might be classified as creative activities, hobbies, things to do alone, or something that involves others. Having something that we love to do helps us get to know ourselves and gives us another way to relax and cope with stress. Such distractions can be useful to forget our anxieties for a while, although they could also have a negative effect by becoming a way of escaping from oneself.

WHAT DO ALL OF THESE PRACTICES HAVE IN COMMON?

1. Bridge inner and outer

All of these practices have the potential to bridge the inner and outer dimensions of life. They all involve the body as well as those invisible parts of you, namely your soul, spirit, and heart. As you may read in the literature on brain research, they also involve both the left and the right brain hemispheres. By participating in any of these, you can develop your whole self, get to know yourself, spend time completely absorbed in something other than the usual work and mental activities. Even people who use practices such as creative work or physical activities only superficially, more like a hobby, will benefit from participating in them. But each of these activities can be engaged in at a deeper level with full awareness of their life-changing possibilities.

2. Include all aspects of yourself

Each practice has a particular focus to develop a part of yourself that needs to be integrated and strengthened. For example, physical activities are important for your body, as they keep you healthy and in good physical shape. Wellness of the body impacts the mind, and vice versa. Reflective reading develops the mind and is important for your spiritual well-being. Creative work is an essential way to develop that other (the right brain) part of you that is often neglected in the administrator's rational–sequential left-brain way of being. Silence, solitude, and meditation are important for reflection and developing an inner focus. Dreamwork is a way to get to know yourself better; psychologists tell us that it gives us insights into our unconscious self. Spending time with friends and family is a way to get in touch with relationships, with how we interact and react to others emotionally, mentally, and physically.

3. Potential for inner development

All of these practices have the potential for an inner focus. When you jog by yourself, you have time to think and reflect. Reading stimulates the mind and helps us to learn to be aware of new habits and behaviors that we may want to initiate. Creative work strengthens our intuition and our problem-solving abilities, and it gives great satisfaction in being able to create a tangible product. When we meditate and listen to the silence within and around, we develop our sense of inner hearing and learn how to be in touch with the present moment. Dreaming is a way to get acquainted with our inner landscapes. Some of these practices, such as creative activities, also have a satisfying outer product, which builds our self-confidence and sense of purpose. Spending time with family and friends causes us to reflect on who we are in relationships with others.

4. Provide choices on the basis of need and interest

Finally, these practices allow choices. Many school administrators I have known tend to be generalists, although some came to administration from a specialty in their teaching, such as physical education or music, or another academic subject. Thus, I believe that this list, which encompasses a variety of activities, will appeal to most school leaders. I suggest that you try and experiment with all of them. You may then decide which you want to include as a regular part of your life. You can choose which one you want to focus on, depending on your self-assessment of what you may need most right now, and depending on which seem to help you the most with your Personal Growth.

GETTING ACQUAINTED WITH THESE PRACTICES

Here are some suggestions to try for a start. You will want to read the subsequent chapters for additional ideas, and to learn more about how these practices will benefit you.

Music: Did you play a musical instrument in high school? Maybe it's sitting in the attic. Maybe your family doesn't even know you play. Pull it out and spend some time with it. If nothing else, it will amuse your children and give you some happy reminiscing. Listening to music is easy—select something relaxing, such as classical music, or one of those nature sound CDs that are intended to make you feel in touch with the ocean or the wind on a rainy day.

Art: You used to draw or paint? Try it again. Find the beauty in nature. Look at a painting with your heart. Go to a museum. Don't analyze or think about what you're seeing, just allow yourself to feel and absorb it. Maybe there is a craft or hobby in which you can become completely engrossed while creating some product, or where you might just enjoy the process without a particular result.

Silence, Solitude, and Meditation: Practice being still now and then and just listen to the birds, or watch a tree grow. Learn to be centered, listening to your heart, even in the midst of a crowd of people. Find some time each day to reflect. Light a candle and meditate; clear your mind.

Dreams: Write down a dream that seems to be staying with you—don't worry about its meaning, just keep track of it. Recollect a day dream you used to have, something you always dreamed of doing. There's still a chance to pursue it. Resurrect it and follow its path.

Physical Activities: Do some kind of physical exercise—anything will do for now. You can decide later which suits you, and which you want to develop into a habit. There are so many options for taking care of your body, including dancing, jogging, yoga, going to the gym, or just taking a walk.

Writing: Get yourself a blank book in which to record your ideas, insights, memories, and reflections. Try a journal, or just use index cards, or make notes in your calendar or on your computer.

Reading: Have at least one inspirational book by your bedside table. Read until you fall asleep—even if it's just a page. Take a novel on your next weekend trip or vacation.

Time With Family and Friends: Spend some time with your children; go to a nice restaurant or a movie with your spouse; listen and talk with friends about your life and their lives, not your work; practice empathy; take a risk and reach out to someone to share your needs; open your heart and welcome a stranger.

Diversions: Do something just for fun! It could even be something considered mundane or routine, such as cleaning the garage, but do it when you feel like doing it and enjoy it. Maintain an inner focus and be completely present in what you do.

REFLECTIONS AND EXERCISES

1. Make a list of the practices from this chapter, each on a separate piece of paper. You may want to divide the category of "creative work" into various activities, such as art, music, or writing. Keep track of when you do each of them. Make notes on how you felt when you did them. How did they help you? What frustrations did you experience?

2. Decide on one of these practices to "play" with for a week. Just be aware of doing something that involves that practice. Have fun with it! Choose another practice for the next week, and so on.

3. At first, try each of these practices superficially, more like a hobby. Then reflect on how you could increase your depth of inner involvement in each. For example, while walking or jogging, try to use all of your senses to be aware of your surroundings and let the sights and sounds enter more deeply into your heart and mind.

4. What does this statement mean to you: "balanced between my head and my heart"? What do you associate with doing things from your head? From your heart? What does being balanced mean to you?

5 Physical Activities: Taking Care of Your Body

When health is absent, wisdom cannot reveal itself, art cannot become manifest, strength cannot be exerted, wealth becomes useless, and reason is powerless.

—Heropilus, 300 B.C.

In studies of school administrators, most of them cited doing some kind of physical exercise at the top of their list of ways to manage stress (Metzger, 2003). The type of physical activities listed by the administrators in my studies included the following: walking, running, biking, working out, exercising, gymnastics, jogging, gardening, walking on a treadmill, hiking, playing golf, yoga, skiing, swimming, horseback riding, dancing, weight lifting, and tennis.

There is no question that administrators understand the value of physical exercise for good health. And there is plenty of evidence about the close connection between good physical health and mental, spiritual, and emotional health. The mind-body connection has been well documented since ancient times, and the scientific evidence supporting this has been continuously mounting (Benson, 1975; Carr, 1974; Karpay, 2000; King, 1981; Sweere, 2004). However, just knowing about the benefits of physical exercise is only the first step to making it a part of your daily life.

Ask yourself these questions:

- How do you view your body: as a partner with your other dimensions of being, or as your enemy?
- Do you treat your body with compassion and respect, or do you seek to hide it?
- Are physical exercise, good nutrition, and enough rest a part of your daily life?
- Is health of mind and body a life commitment for you?

In this chapter we will look at some ways you can take care of your physical health, particularly through exercise. Then we will make the connection to your Personal Growth and conclude with some practical suggestions for using the "path" of physical activities as a way to relax, renew yourself, and keep a balance in your life.

PHYSICAL EXERCISE AS A PART OF GOOD HEALTH

George was overweight and he knew it. But somehow the resolution to do something about it was always one step beyond him—somewhere in the hoped-for future. George knew when it all began. He was in fairly good shape when he first became an assistant principal. His work excited him. There was never a boring moment and he felt needed. His principal was somewhat of a workaholic, so George developed some bad health habits as well. He ate his lunch on the run, often just something starchy or a bite of fast food. He worked late most days and didn't feel like doing anything except mindless TV-watching when he got home. He'd let his membership to the gym lapse. "No time now that I'm an administrator," he told his two best friends with whom he used to go jogging early in the mornings at least twice a week.

It took a mild heart attack to wake George up. When I recently saw him, 6 months afterwards, he was proud to tell me he'd started exercising again and was watching his food intake. George had lost weight and looked great. He beamed as he told me that he felt so lucky and grateful for his second chance to get that part of his life in order.

Do you know someone like George? Talk with him or her. Allow your friend's experience to increase your own motivation for getting serious about building physical exercise into your life. People who have had such a wake-up call often can't wait to talk about it and share their new attitude and way of life with others.

Our modern lifestyle with its technological advances saves us time and energy, and lets us do things faster and more efficiently. But the price we have paid is the loss of physical activity with a disastrous impact on our health. In 1960, President John F. Kennedy enacted the President's Council on Physical Fitness to address this issue. Dr. Kenneth Cooper's *Aerobics,* published in 1968, became the springboard for the creation of a variety of activities intent on keeping us active and fit. Despite such efforts, however, heart disease, stroke, cancer, and accidents are now the leading causes of death in the United States (Karpay, 2000). These are related to lifestyle and could be reduced through physical fitness.

Here is a list of benefits of physical exercise (Karpay, 2000, pp. 10–12). You probably already know these, but read them again as a reminder:

1. improved respiration, cardiac output, vascular system

2. increased muscular strength, endurance, and bone density

3. improved flexibility, sensory skills, bowel function, and psychological effect

4. enhanced social experiences with friends and loved ones

Most importantly, physical exercise will make you feel better. Next to physical exercise, most health experts list good nutrition and getting adequate rest as other components of good physical health. Particular activities that are often associated with relieving stress include sports, games, yoga, tai chi, meditation, guided progressive relaxation, and sleep (Karpay, 2000, p. 237).

CONNECTING PHYSICAL EXERCISE WITH PERSONAL GROWTH

In his book *Golden Rules for Vibrant Health in Body, Mind, and Spirit,* Joseph Sweere (2004) advocates a holistic approach to health and wellness. He emphasizes the importance of true health care instead of disease management and states that it is never too late to begin your journey toward improved health and better quality of life.

Another author (Yehling, 2004) states that overwhelming evidence from cellular and energetic medicine supports the ancient spiritual masters' contention that our bodies are the intelligence and spiritual centers of our being:

The individual who operates from strong mind/body awareness enjoys a steady flow of vitality and treats the body as a finely tuned organism from which all life experience emanates. The mind creates the body just as the body determines the state of the mind. (p. 25)

Awareness of the body is the first step in most relaxation techniques. In the subsequent chapters on meditation and creative work, you will find some exercises for breathing and noting the flow of sensations in your body as a way to lead into these other practices.

The practice of yoga has been used frequently to develop greater awareness of the mind-body connection. *Yoga* is a Sanskrit word meaning "unification" (with the divine). Yoga improves flexibility, aids in relaxation, improves circulation, and increases energy. Certain styles can also improve muscular strength and endurance (Carr, 1974; Farhi, 2000; Karpay, 2000; Lasater, 1995). Renowned yoga teacher Gary Kraftsow (1999) describes this relationship superbly well:

As human beings, we are a complex of interrelated systems (including the various components of our anatomy, physiology, and psychology) existing within a larger complex of interrelated systems, including our interpersonal relationships and our environment. There is a reciprocal relation between these various structural components and the metabolic functioning of the body as a whole . . . the key to health lies in the balanced interaction of all these systems. (p. xvi)

Physical exercises not only help the body, but are a way to give rest to your mind and provide time for you to become aware of the voices from your inner self. For example, as you are walking, jogging, or exercising, your mind is free to roam, your senses are free to take in your environment, your creative, intuitive self has time to evolve ideas, you give your spiritual dimension an opportunity to unfold, unhindered by active thoughts of a particular task to be done at that time. You are just walking, jogging, stretching, biking, swimming—doing something wonderful for your body and allowing these exercises to become part of your journey to wholeness.

CHOOSING A PHYSICAL ACTIVITY

Let's review what some of your choices might be for getting in shape through physical activities. Most experts agree that physical fitness includes the following elements: cardiorespiratory fitness, muscular strength and endurance, flexibility, and rest and recovery (Karpay, 2000). Various types of exercises meet these goals. For example, aerobic exercise is great for cardiorespiratory fitness; stretching exercises for flexibility; and strength training exercise such as weight training, strength training machines, and calisthenics for muscular improvement.

When considering what exercise you want to select, use these questions as criteria for making your choice:

- How much time are you willing to allot for exercise?
- What are some good times of the day or week for you when you could build in a time for exercise? Experts recommend doing physical exercise at least three times a week, for 20–60 minutes each time.
- Do you prefer to exercise indoors or outdoors, or some of each?
- What types of activities can you do indoors? You may want to use a video workout program tape that includes all the elements of physical fitness. This may work well for you because you can do it at home and at times that are convenient for you. It also takes less preparation and effort than going to a gym.

You may prefer the discipline of going to a health club or gym, or taking classes with others. You may also use equipment at home, such as a treadmill, stationary bike, NordicTrack, or stair-climbing machines. Strength training may include weights, bands and tubes, and isometric exercises. A medicine ball or doing Pilates is also a favored activity for at-home exercising. Pilates is a system of gentle strength-training physical exercise started by Joseph Pilates that has become increasingly popular in recent years (Karpay, 2000).

If you prefer outdoor exercises, you might choose walking, jogging, running, bicycling, hiking, swimming, or winter sports such as downhill or cross-country skiing and skating. Some of my friends even tell me that playing golf is good physical exercise, provided they don't ride in a cart.

The benefits of just walking are consistently lauded by most fitness experts. National attention was given to walking with a Walk to Work Day on April 2, 2004, sponsored by the U.S. Department of Health and Human Services in cooperation with *Prevention* magazine.

Exercising Alone or With Others

A friend of mine has a regular Saturday morning walk with a group of three or four other women. After their exercise, they chat over a nutritious breakfast and catch up on each others' lives. It works well for their bodies and their spirits. Maybe you like to play a team sport with others. Just be careful to remember your limits, and don't get hurt trying to show off what you used to do in your youth. Do it—not for competition, but for yourself! If you like to exercise alone, there are plenty of choices for you as well. Many of the indoor and outdoor activities listed above can be done by yourself or with others.

Particular Skills, Techniques, or Equipment

If you want to learn a particular sport, such as skiing, try taking lessons. You're never too old to learn, and you may even win a championship or run in a marathon if that is your goal. I love downhill skiing perhaps more than any other of my physical exercises. I love the feel of challenging myself, of the brisk air in my face, and becoming one with the magnificent mountain world as I look out from the top of a slope. A sport you enjoy doing can refresh and renew you in many ways.

Cost

Joining a health club or buying equipment can get expensive, but may be worth the investment if that will keep you going. If you can afford it, the ultimate luxury might be to hire a personal trainer to guide you!

DEVELOPING A HABIT

This is perhaps the most important section of this chapter. Awareness that you need to build physical exercise into your routine is the first step. Overcoming excuses is the second step. Making a plan, a commitment, and staying with it is the most important step.

The following suggestions may be helpful to you as you become serious about making physical exercise a part of your life.

1. Take up informal daily exercise.

Think of opportunities throughout your day to be more physically active and aware of improving your health. This includes watching the food you put into your body and making sure you get plenty of rest. You can add exercise to your daily life in simple ways, such as intentionally parking your car farther away from your destination to increase walking time, properly stretching your muscles as you do your daily chores, sitting with awareness of what's good for your back to avoid back problems, and using exercise as transportation. Now and then try riding your bicycle to do errands or, if feasible, walk or ride your bike to work.

2. Develop one formal exercise practice.

Decide on one thing you will do three times a week to be more physically active. Choose one that meets your needs based on criteria such as those suggested above. Then make a schedule and build it into your day and week. Review chapter 3 for how to find time. It is important that the activity you choose is something you already enjoy, something that is fun and convenient for you. Make an appointment with yourself to do it.

If you can't decide what to chose, begin with walking. A walk can be invigorating and a good way to clear your head of anxious thoughts. Your body is working and your soul is resting. This allows ideas to arise from deeper within you about what you want your life to be like, what is important to you. New insights are free to emerge for problems to which you have sought answers. Walking will help you to gain a better perspective on life by being present to each moment of your exercise.

3. Begin slowly and reward yourself.

Start with a short-term commitment and gradually increase. Be gentle with yourself if at times you don't stick to your goal. Don't scold yourself. Just pick right up the next week. Give yourself rewards when you've stayed with it. Buy a pair of new walking shoes. Celebrate with your family. Document your achievements. Reflect on when you've missed your exercise program—but don't become anxious about it. Just dwell on it long enough to learn from it. Keep a wellness calendar. For your long-term goal to be more physically fit, you could do some visualization to imagine yourself in your new body—feeling really great—maybe running that marathon!

Stay with the day-to-day small steps. Long-term goals and lofty motivations are always more difficult to achieve. When I was principal, I had a fifth grade teacher who complained constantly about her students being unmotivated to study and learn, even though she said that she continuously told them about the benefits of a good education to their future careers. This same teacher was overweight and not physically fit. I wanted so much to tell her that she was just like her students—unable to make the connection between her own future health and the food she ate today, and unable to see the impact of her lack of physical exercise on her well-being in years to come.

4. Exercise properly.

Ellen Karpay (2000) has developed a nice and compact model to remember that she calls the F-I-T-T principles of exercise. They involve

Frequency, Intensity, Time, and the Type of exercise. Apply these principles to all elements of your exercise program. To achieve desired results and continue to improve, adjust the Frequency (how often you exercise), the Intensity (how hard you exercise), the Time (how long you exercise), and the Type of exercise you do. This will help you to stay motivated, to improve, to stay balanced, and to continue to have some degree of enjoyment in your exercise.

Fitness begins in your mind, with your awareness. Then you develop a new habit—one step at a time. Finally, you couldn't live without it. At first it will require effort and self-discipline. But in time you will learn to depend on your exercise times to help you integrate what's good for your body and your mind. It will be more of a pleasure (most of the time), not just a chore. On those days when it seems like a duty, just keep telling yourself that this is good for you and that you deserve it!

Your exercise will give you time to visualize a goal or rehearse an affirmation for a change you want to make in your life. You will learn to focus on your breath and know that it fills your body with new life. Physical exercise is a way to good health—body, soul, and spirit. You will forget perfection as a goal, remembering that fitness is always a work in progress, as is the inner work you are doing while exercising.

REFLECTIONS AND EXERCISES

1. Make a list of reasons why you are not practicing some physical exercise. Then give yourself a healthy response to each. Select one of your reasons and responses to work on for this week.

2. At the end of the day, reflect on how you are building more physical exercise into your life just by informally adjusting some of your habits. Here are some simple ways:
   - Walk rather than ride.
   - Use stairs rather than the elevator.
   - Stretch your arms as you reach for something and lift items correctly to gain flexibility.
   - Do neck stretches as you sit in an airplane or as a passenger in a car, at your desk, or at any time.
   - Do isometric exercise (e.g., with your buttocks, thighs, or upper arms) as you sit in a meeting.
   - If you're waiting near a curb or some stairs, go up and down a few times to exercise your calves.

3. Subscribe to a journal such as *Prevention* or *Spirituality & Health* or a fitness magazine to stay motivated and current with fitness ideas.

Look on Web sites of associations and organizations who advocate good health (e.g., the American College of Sports Medicine).

4. Buy a book on good nutrition and become more aware of what you put into your body. Learn about what's new in nutrition. Establish healthy eating as a part of your lifestyle—for the rest of your life (no more dieting)!

5. Join a yoga class, a gym, or buy a video for home use. Read one of the books on good health referred to in this chapter.

6 Reflective Reading: Nourishing Your Spirit and Soul

I cannot live without books.

—Thomas Jefferson

Of the many gifts of the world that can lead us to contemplation, to creative reverie, to quiet moment of being in the present, perhaps books are the most powerful.

—Kundtz, 2000, p. 144

THE MOUNTAIN OF TOO MUCH TO READ

Principal Steve is staring at his stack of professional journals. He quickly closes the drawer where he's piled them.

Then his eyes fall on the heap of memos and letters in the in-basket on his desk. These should be read today.

Steve sighs. He turns around.

Looking at his computer reminds him of the electronic newsletter from his assistant superintendent that came in the e-mail yesterday. He hasn't read that, nor the 45 e-mail messages he will get today. They really should do something about spam mail!

He gets up from his desk chair and wanders over to a picture on his wall. It's a picture of Abraham Lincoln, for whom his school was named.

He used to love to read biographies, but now there is just too much else to read. The only reading he seems to be able to get to, besides the necessary professional materials, is his books on tape on the way home from work.

He turns his back to his desk and walks out of his office. Right now he just needs to get out and search for the smile of a first grader out on the playground.

Have you experienced the frustration of having too much to read, of not being able to find time to read what you really want to read? One of the consequences of the information explosion has been the increasing quantity of materials to read. Administrators need to know speed-reading techniques. They need to know how to glance at reading materials and quickly decide what to toss, and what to read carefully. Writers of memos need to be more aware of their readers' needs and write in shorter paragraphs with the main idea in the first sentences.

WHAT ARE YOUR READING HABITS?

As a school administrator, you basically have two kinds of reading materials:

- that which you have to read, such as professional journals, memoranda, e-mails related to work, laws and regulations, policies, and textbooks
- that which you'd like to read, but for which you may have trouble finding time, including biographies, novels, poems, short stories, spiritual books, news journals and magazines, self-help books, and books or magazines related to your hobbies and interests

Are you like Principal Steve, who has difficulty making time for reading, especially something you would like to read? Here are some ideas for enhancing your recreational reading habits.

1. Always have a book by your bedside and read something before you fall asleep.

2. Try reading a selection in the morning, maybe along with, or instead of reading the morning newspaper or watching the TV news.

3. You might take something with you to read as you have lunch—when you can eat alone.

4. If your school or district has an SSR (Sustained Silent Reading) or other similar program for students, participate in that. You'll be a good role model for your staff and students.

5. Divide your reading materials into stacks by type of reading, such as professional journals, personal magazines, self-knowledge/spiritual books, and recreational reading. Then, depending on your frame of mind and how you're feeling, you can quickly select something suitable from a stack.

6. Always take something to read with you to appointments—it's a great way to fill waiting times.

7. You might join a book club, or even start one at your workplace. Members take turns recommending a book for all to read and discuss. One of my superintendent friends selected *Leading With Soul* (Bolman & Deal, 1995) to read with all of his administrators and reported great results.

8. Weekends or trips are good to find longer times for reading.

9. Use an audio version of a book on tape, or a CD, as you commute in your car.

10. As with all other Personal Growth activities, developing a habit requires a determined desire to do it. "Make it a priority," as some administrators have told me. "Make it a part of your routine!"

BENEFITS OF RECREATIONAL AND REFLECTIVE READING

In their classic guide, *How to Read a Book* (Adler & Van Doren, 1972), the authors distinguish various levels of reading: elementary reading (basic word-for-word reading), inspectional reading (including speed-reading and skimming material), analytical reading (for understanding and information), and syntopical reading (comparing, synthesizing, evaluating).

The administrator's professional reading would primarily be at the first three levels—basic reading, skimming for information and for understanding, and analytical reading. Administrators need to know how to do their jobs better and be familiar with the most current rules and procedures so that they can avoid making too many mistakes. Their job survival depends on this kind of reading.

Unfortunately, that kind of reading doesn't generally address the inner and personal needs of the administrator. Harold Bloom (2000) in *How to Read and Why* states that "the sorrow of professional reading is that you recapture only rarely the pleasure of reading you knew in youth" (p. 22).

The main purpose of this chapter is to talk about another kind of reading: reading just for you—for enjoyment, for insights, for Personal Growth. This kind of reading, for pleasure, for re-creation of your spirit and soul, might be included in Adler and Van Doren's highest level, syntopical reading.

"Ultimately we read in order to strengthen the self," Bloom (2000) stated, in citing Bacon, Johnson, and Emerson, and when "reading falls apart . . . much of the self scatters with it" (pp. 22–23). That's a poetic way of saying that reading (especially the recreational kind) is something you need to do to keep yourself together. In other words, reading is an important way to engage in your Personal Growth.

The act of reading and of contemplation share many of the same characteristics. Nancy Malone (2004) writes about the spirituality of reading: "Both are usually done alone, in silence and physical stillness, our attention focused, our whole selves—body, mind, and hearts—engaged" (p. 8).

Through recreational and inspirational reading you can gain wisdom to live a better life. Such reading can be a nice getaway when you don't have time to do so in real life. We read about other people and their lives to learn about ours. Our lives are changed by what we read. We read imaginative literature, such as folktales, myths, or science fiction so that we can touch something beyond ourselves—something of the traditions and symbols of other people and other epochs of the past and future of human history. We find ourselves in novels and, after spending a few hours with one, we feel that we've been away for a long time. Reading gives us new perspectives on our immediate situation. Through reading we meet our companions of the spirit, as one author calls them (Versluis, 2004).

We don't have enough time in our lives to meet enough people, to learn enough from personal experiences. Books help us to get to know ourselves and the world. As we share in the lives of others and reflect on their experiences, we learn more about the way things are. Spiritual books, in particular, help us to develop our inner dimensions. They can give us a sense of spiritual uplifting and can provide impetus for changing our beliefs and actions.

Serge King (1981) advocates reading as a way of incorporating healthy new beliefs into your system. He states that "when you read something interesting, you automatically go into an altered state of consciousness that resembles meditation" (p. 109). King cautions, however, that one reading of a book, no matter how moving it may be, is generally not enough to alter a habitual belief system. He also recommends enhancing the effectiveness of reading in terms of beneficial changes in one's beliefs by doing some kind of a relaxation exercise before you start to read.

You may want to do more reading about the practice of bibliotherapy, which has been used as a method of therapy in particular with children and adolescents. Even for adults, getting into the characters of a story helps to verbalize feelings, work through problems, and improve your life (Stanley, 1999). Bibliodrama is a similar technique that has been used and made known by scholar Peter A. Pitzele of the Jewish Theological Seminary in New York and chairman of the advisory board of the Institute for Contemporary Midrash.

TRY THIS TECHNIQUE FOR READING REFLECTIVELY

There is an ancient practice developed by Benedictine monks (Kaisch, 1994) called *lectio divina,* meaning "divine reading." It is a way of reading that allows you to experience a passage from within, a contemplative practice of reading.

The four steps of *lectio divina* were originally intended for spiritual reading and were used mainly for reading sacred scriptures. Whether you relate this type of reading to a religious practice is completely your personal choice. However, this technique is a useful one and may be adapted to other readings as a way to read more reflectively.

Lectio divina has four parts: *lectio, meditatio, oratio,* and *contemplatio.* In practice these four divisions flow naturally into one another and not always in the order suggested.

Exercise for Reflective Reading:

Lectio: Select a short passage from a book on which you want to reflect. Let your mind and body settle into quietness. Read the passage with an inner listening, not only with your mind, but with your heart. Be open and receptive. What does this passage have to say to you?

Meditatio: Reflect, meditate on the passage. Read it again and again, slowly. Which part, a word or phrase, speaks to you? Focus on that and repeat those words or phrases. What is their deepest meaning? Let the words teach you directly, in your heart.

Oratio: As you enter the passage by reading and meditating, what is your inner response? What touches you about it? How are you moved? What is working inside you? Spontaneously express your response through words or feelings. You may want to write something at this point or just mentally acknowledge what is happening in response to your reading.

Contemplatio: Finally, contemplate the passage. Sit in silence and simply flow with whatever appears. Let yourself rest here—sitting a while without words. This step of not-doing is hardest, but important in order to explore your being. Trust that something is happening in your heart, an insight, an inner change that will manifest itself somewhere in your life.

GETTING THE MOST OUT OF YOUR READING

If you're reading a novel or short story you may just read and take in the totality of the story. If you're reading a book that provides insights, wisdom, practical suggestions, you may want to underline, make notes in margins, or—my favorite practice—write a page number and a key word or phrase on the inside back cover pages for future reference. I often go back to such books and look up the pages I've noted on various topics and the sections I had underlined in my first reading.

Whatever method of keeping notes on your reading you choose, it will help to make your reading come alive to you. You can go back to such books periodically and read just the highlighted parts. You might even try the 17th century method of the commonplace book (Versluis, 2004), which consisted of memorable quotations and aphorisms. Such a book was set in a common place, such as a library, where various readers could contribute. You and others who read the same book, such as members of your book club or a special friend, might all contribute observations and thoughts from your readings for later reflections. You might try this technique with your book club or reading group.

Here is a method I have used for making notes to retrieve your favorite journal articles: If you like to keep the complete journal, write on the front page of the magazine the page number and a key word of something you may want to look up later. You may also want to tear apart journals or magazines and keep certain articles for future reference. Of course, it is important to have a good filing system of categories and subjects that reflects your interests. But the filing system should be simple and focused (a friend of mine just saved his journals for a particular year in a box). In saving materials, you will want to limit yourself to those you might not easily be able to find elsewhere in the future, or to which you need immediate access. The Internet today has made looking up things easier, but I still value the books and journals I've read and saved. Upon revisiting them, I am always surprised to discover new meanings for my current life situation in the notes from my past readings. And more than once, I found a favorite article that was just what a friend or colleague or one of my students needed.

WHAT ARE SOME GOOD BOOKS AND WHERE CAN I FIND THEM?

When you are able to find those precious few minutes or hours to read something other than your work-related material, you probably want to read something that someone else has recommended. I know that I'm always asking my friends to recommend a good book they've read.

In the Resource notes for this chapter I have included a list of my favorite Personal Growth books that you may want to read. These are the ones I have found most valuable in my own Personal Growth journey. Books related to specific practices are also mentioned in the various chapters of this book.

You can browse in your neighborhood bookstore in sections such as self-help, relationships, health, psychology, religion, and many other similar categories. There are also catalogs available that you may want to look through for Personal Growth books, videos, and CDs, such as Shambhala Publications (the leading publisher on Buddhism and Taoism in English), Sounds True ("Wisdom for the Inner Life"), Explorations ("Visions of the Past, Memories of the Future"), One Spirit ("Resources for the Spirit, Mind, and Body"), and Parabola ("Myth, Tradition, and the Search for Meaning"). Most of these will have a Web site for you to look up. You will find sections in these with the following types of intriguing topics: nature, creativity, art, martial arts, religion and philosophy, yoga, health and healing, cooking, resources for balanced living, tools for your total well-being, your quest for the divine within, wisdom from the cultures of the world, conscious journey—the pursuit of deeper meaning, various meditation traditions, and how writing can save your life.

Here are some good magazines with a variety of topics related to Personal Growth that you might want to locate: *Spirituality & Health: The Soul/Body Connection, Prevention, Science and Spirit, Parabola: The Search for Meaning, What is Enlightenment: Redefining Spirituality for an Evolving World,* and *Weavings: A Journal of the Christian Spiritual Life.*

REFLECTIONS AND EXERCISES

1. What is the best book you've read this past year? What do you remember from it? What one or two central ideas have impacted your life as a result of reading that book? Write a reflection in your journal. Do the same with your other books.

2. Make a commitment to purchase one of the spiritual books listed in the Resource notes for this chapter. Make a plan to read at least one page or section each day.

3. Practice doing a relaxation exercise before your reading time. Try this simple breathing technique. Sit comfortably and become aware of your breath. With each in-breath, repeat the words "breathing in." As you breathe out, repeat "breathing out." Feel the breath fill your body as it comes in, and "watch" it going out through your extremities. Do this four times, breathing slowly and deeply, but naturally. Then begin your reading.

4. Take a look at your bookshelves. Walk back and forth and read the spines of books you've read. Reminisce a moment with a book as you would with an old friend. What memories does it evoke? Review those in your stack that you want to read and put one on top that you want to begin.

7 Music, Art, Writing, and Other Creative Work: Engaging Transformative Powers

One ought, every day at least, to hear a little song, read a good poem, see a fine picture, and, if it were possible, to speak a few reasonable words.

—Johann Wolfgang Goethe

The greatness of an artist lies in the building of an inner world, and in the ability to reconcile this inner world with the outer.

—Albert Einstein

More has been written about the powerful potential of creative activities as a path for Personal Growth than probably any other of the practices described in this book, with the possible exception of meditation. In this chapter I am including all types of creative activities: music, art, writing, and a variety of other activities listed in the creative category by administrators. One of the surprising findings of my research was that creative activities were not used very frequently by school administrators (see figures in chapter 4 Resource notes).

WHAT KIND OF CREATIVE ACTIVITIES DO ADMINISTRATORS USE?

I will begin with a brief review of the types of creative activities used most by the administrators who responded in my surveys and interviews. Superintendents and deans used music (mainly listening to it) more frequently than other types of creative work. Music was ranked third highest of the nine categories provided, whereas writing and creative work ranked as the least of the practices used. In the studies involving mostly principals and beginning-level administrators, creative work was ranked second and third lowest.

In the category of creative work, administrators listed a variety of activities, including those that would commonly be described as art (ceramics, painting, drawing, sculpture), but also the following: projects around the house, yard work, crossword puzzles, photography, building dollhouses, photography, Web design, scrapbooking, and sewing.

In the category of "other (diversions)," administrators also included lists of what might be classified as creative work. In other words, what some administrators viewed as a diversion, others saw as creative work. Examples of such activities included fixing things, gardening, knitting, home decorating, filmmaking, and cross-stitching.

The category for a particular activity is less important than how an activity is used as a way to balance life, as a way to engage time that involves the Creative Spirit, as Adriana Diaz (1992) calls it. Diaz guides her readers to find the potential for healing wounds of negative self-image through drawing and painting. She emphasizes that the creative process needs our wholeness, body and soul. Creative work involves all of our time and energy while we are engaged in it.

The connections made by the administrators in my studies between various types of creative activities and their Personal Growth have been confirmed by some recent books with intriguing titles, such as *Zen and the Art of Knitting* (Murphy, 2002), in which the author explores the links between knitting, spirituality, and creativity. Another author (Versluis, 2004) wrote a book entitled *Awakening the Contemplative Spirit: Writing, Gardening and the Inner Life,* likening cultivation of a garden to contemplative spiritual practices, which included writing and reading.

CREATIVITY AND ART

When I first became a principal, I was advised that it wasn't a good idea to get too close to any of my teachers. Personal friendships would tempt me to share confidential information, and would make others think that I had favorites. I don't know if this was good advice, but I was always a bit guarded about friendships with members of the staff.

My art teacher, Kathryn, became as close a friend as I thought a principal was allowed to have. She actively reminded me of another side of my administrator's life—the importance of looking at things through an artist's eyes, and through the eyes of children creating something beautiful. I was drawn to her gentle and positive spirit, and visited her room whenever my administrative duties became a bit too stressful. She would show me a finger painting with the proud artist beaming up at me as I admired his work.

When I left the school, Kathryn gave me a framed painting of a blue elephant by a second-grade boy, Peter. She had written a note on the back of it for me to always remember children, art, love, and to take time. Kathryn died shortly after that, but Peter's picture has hung in my office through all of my positions for many years.

I recently gave the elephant picture with Kathryn and Peter's legacy to a young woman friend when she got her first teaching job. I hope that this little work of art will live on as a symbol of the important balance that creativity provides in our busy lives, and as a memory of a child who intuitively knew this.

Tap Your Magic Within

I have wondered why creative work was used so infrequently by administrators in my studies as a practice for their Personal Growth. Certainly, further research would be needed to answer this question. Perhaps it is that many administrators don't consider themselves artists or creative. Or maybe it's because many of these activities do require more time, and finding time is undoubtedly the greatest challenge to engaging in any of these activities.

Writers on creativity agree that everyone has creative abilities that can be developed. There is also no question as to the power of creative work to "tap the magic and wisdom within" (Diaz, 1983). Could it be that, in today's educational environment, where the rewards are focused on rigidly raising academic standards, creativity is no longer valued as much? Are the arts seen as "dispensable luxuries that must prove their worth in the impersonal mass market" (Csikszentmihalyi, 1996, p. 11)?

Here is what some of the many writers on creativity have said about the subject as it relates to the impact on the individual—that is, the value of creative work for Personal Growth.

In his book *Out of Our Minds: Learning to Be Creative,* Ken Robinson (2001) raises this issue and states that "one of the legacies of academicism is the exile of feeling from education. Reconnecting feeling and intellect is vital for the development of human resources and for the promotion of creativity" (p. 14). Other writers have pointed out that the intellect is often associated with the hard sciences and feelings with the soft arts. I wonder what the impact of this myth has been on the profession of educational administration.

Best known for his work on the psychology of flow, Mihaly Csikszentmihalyi (1996) conducted research on creativity. He describes it as a process that unfolds over a lifetime, "even though personal creativity may not lead to fame and fortune, it can do something that to the individual's point of view is even more important: make day-to-day experiences more vivid, more enjoyable, more rewarding" (p. 344). He talks about liberating the creative energy of wonder and awe in all domains of life.

A direct connection is made by Van Dusen (1999) between beauty, wonder, and the mystical mind, in his book by that title. He defines art as whatever someone finds beautiful and calls it a process of continual discovery: "With each discovery, I expand contact with and understand my inner self" (p. 70).

Creativity is a prerogative of humans, according to many writers. Arieti (1976) believes that creative work has a dual role. It enlarges the universe by adding or uncovering new dimensions, and it enriches and expands the person, who will be able to experience these new dimensions inwardly (p. 5). Arieti also emphasizes how creativity exists not only in a work of art or a creative product, but in all dimensions of human endeavor and inquiry, including scientific pursuits.

Best-selling author and workshop leader Julia Cameron (1992) describes the artist's way as "in essence, a spiritual path, initiated and practiced through creativity" (p. xi). She believes that creativity is our true nature, through which we make spiritual contact: "We undertake certain spiritual exercises to achieve alignment with the creative energy of the universe" (p. 1). By engaging in creative work, she shows how we can recover a sense of safety, identity, power, integrity, possibility, abundance, connection, strength, compassion, self-protection (e.g., from workaholism), autonomy, and faith. Interspersed with quotes, affirmations, and exercises, this book is a must-get for developing and using your creativity.

Finally, here is a quote from another writer to confirm the importance and value of creative work. It is from Peter London's book (1989), *No More Secondhand Art: Awakening the Artist Within.* He talks about the transformative powers of art as an essential step toward uncovering our original selves. One of the most profound functions of art has to do with

> personal and collective empowerment, personal growth, commu-
> nion with this world, and the search for what lies beneath and
> above this world . . . through the creative encounter we seek to
> facilitate our private and communal evolution so that we may
> become who we prefer to be. (pp. 4–5)

Doing Creative Work for Your Personal Growth

If you feel inspired by reading what these authors have said and want to develop your creativity as a path for your own Personal Development, here are some suggestions.

1. Identify an area of interest.

Select something that you feel allows you to release your creativity. It should be something you enjoy, something that can give you the satisfaction of original work, something that could fill you with wonder and excitement. Perhaps you can resurrect a hobby you used to have, maybe an "arts and crafts" project. Look at the lists mentioned above from other administrators and see if something suits you. A visit to your school's kindergarten room might give you ideas. Even with the current emphasis on accountability and academics, you might still find an atmosphere of free expression there, a culture in which creativity is encouraged.

2. Consciously get involved in it.

Whatever you selected, perhaps doing some creative home decorating, gardening, photography, painting, sewing, or making something for a grand-child, give yourself to it as completely as possible. This means setting aside a time for it and stilling your mind so that you don't think about the hundred other things you might or should be doing. As I suggested in connection with reflective reading in chapter 6, you might want to do a relax-ation technique before beginning. This time should consciously be set aside for your Personal Growth, not as an activity to hurry through in order to get to the real business of your life.

3. Give your whole self to the activity.

This means body, soul, and spirit! In other words, pour yourself into the activity and become completely absorbed in it. Let your body be comfortable in a relaxed surrounding, a space conducive to what you are doing. Be aware of your feelings as you engage in your project. Perhaps you feel inadequate about the product, perhaps you wonder if it will be good enough. Go into such feelings and acknowledge them. Then raise your awareness to feel gratitude for being in this space, doing this thing that you have chosen to do, here and now. Enjoy even a small part of what you're doing that seems to work well—perhaps a color that you've selected that harmonizes well with another. Just allow your thoughts and feelings to arise and be as they are. If you're sad, be sad for a little while; if memories arise, be with them and then watch them pass. It is important that your activity allows you to get to know and experience whatever part of yourself it evokes.

4. Own the product as a reflection of you.

This means that the real value of your product resides in the experience you are having. In creative involvement, it is truly the process that is more important. You will feel proud of some of what you did, and you may feel inadequate about other parts of it. Other people looking at your product may make some comments. Tell yourself that their reactions are not as important as what you experienced. Take a few moments at the end of your activity to reflect on your feelings and on what you learned about yourself during this time. How does this work reflect you? What surprised you? What did you enjoy about it? What did you hate about it? What went particularly well? What about it lifted your spirits? You may want to sit down for a few minutes afterwards and write down what you experienced.

MUSIC

Principal Randy was a former actor and music major. He has a delightful communication style and a positive attitude about life. He is a great speaker, and the children in Randy's 1,000-plus inner city school love his enthusiasm in assemblies and in his personal interactions. As his superintendent personally told me, Randy is an outstanding principal. Randy confessed to me how difficult it was for him to find time for himself during the school day. However, in observing him, I could see how his creativity was expressed in many ways as leader of his school, in the way he solved problems, made decisions, and interacted with people. Even though his career as a performer was in the past, he still attends plays and musical performances and finds needed renewal in such activities. Not surprisingly, Randy is a strong advocate for music and arts in his school and district.

The Mozart Effect and Other Merits of Music

Here are some ways listed by administrators for how they used music as a practice for their Personal Development: listening to jazz or folk; attending symphony; listening to the radio (e.g., National Public Radio) while driving or as background music; playing a musical instrument; songwriting; playing in musical groups. These musical activities cover everything from being a participant in making music to listening to various kinds of music.

The power and impact of music have been well documented in a number of books. Among the best known is Don Campbell's (1997) *The Mozart Effect: Tapping the Power of Music to Heal the Body, Strengthen the Mind, and Unlock the Creative Spirit*. Campbell, who founded the Institute of Music, Health, and Education, coined the term *Mozart Effect*. He provides specific evidence on the life-changing effects of sound, various types of music, and other forms of vibration on health, learning, and behavior. He summarizes his work simply in these words: "Music is good for you— physically, emotionally, and spiritually" (inside cover page). His studies showed, for example, that students who sing or play an instrument scored up to 51 points higher on SATs than the national average. His research included the calming and healing impact of music on expectant mothers and hospital patients. This is a powerful book and a must-read on this topic.

Another work that explores how music opens the mind, affects the brain, and takes us to the threshold of ecstasy is *Music, the Brain, and Ecstasy: How Music Captures our Imagination* (Jourdain, 1997). The author analyzes scientific evidence about musical psychoacoustics, which is the study of how minds perceive sound and music. He reports on the impact of all aspects of musical perception and performance, including tone, melody, harmony, rhythm, composition performance, listening, understanding, and ecstasy.

The Musician's Soul (Jordan, 1999) examines spirituality in music for performers, teachers, composers, conductors, and music educators. The author introduces the book with these words, "The journey of this book is about one idea: you must trust, believe, and love yourself . . . and others" (p. 7). Whereas music-making is constructed of correct notes, rhythms, dynamics, articulation, he calls these human qualities the mortar of music. He discusses three important ingredients to making music: being open, being vulnerable, and knowing your center.

In a summary of his new book about the 17th century German astronomer and mathematician Johannes Kepler, Conner (2004) says that Kepler found expressions of harmony in geometry, music, and astronomy.

Kepler felt that it was in music that "perfect harmonies best touch the senses. Here we feel them, see them, listen to them" (p. 72).

And finally, *The Inner Game of Music* is one in a series coauthored by Timothy Gallwey, who also wrote the popular *Inner Game* books about tennis, skiing, and golf. Gallwey worked together with noted musician Barry Green (Green & Gallwey, 1986) to write this interesting book. As the title implies, there are an outer and an inner game that have impact on one another. The authors emphasize that it is the success in the inner game that is the deciding factor between success and failure in the outer game: "As we turn to examine the inner world, with its teeming doubts and hopes and expectations, we need to know just what is going on inside us" (p. 12).

Music for Your Personal Growth

1. Make music a part of your life.

Whether you are a listener, like to sing, or play an instrument, make time for it in your life. Even if you play music in the background of another activity, select the kind of music that enhances what you are in the process of doing. Personally, I love classical music, but there are times when perhaps jazz, folk music, or another style provides the best background music. When a piece is played that touches your heart in a particular way, stop for a few seconds and give that music your complete attention—without neglecting your main activity of course, such as driving on a freeway.

Don't die with your music still inside you, to paraphrase Oliver Wendell Holmes ("Many people die with their music still in them," he said). So, make your music!

2. Make music a part of your conscious Personal Development.

Set aside times to listen fully and allow your complete attention to be present to the music. Really listen and hear it! Let it go inside you and have an impact on you. For example, when you go to a concert, or just listen to a CD, listen without analysis and judgment. Feel the sound, the rhythm of the music and let it heal you inside. Feel the emotions, or the lack of them, as you listen. Allow pain and sadness, or joy and ecstasy to arise. Simply be aware—allow the music to have some impact inside you.

If you are a performer, whether singing or playing an instrument, become completely involved in making the music. I play several instruments—none of them professionally. As a lesson of what not to do, I painfully remember many years ago when I took my harpsichord to church to play a selection. Somewhere in the midst of playing, I made a mistake. It was months before I played again. Now I know how sad and limiting my reaction was to this mistake. I guess I should have read *The Inner Game* book sooner. Now when I play, I am aware of my inner perfectionist. I am more accepting of that part of me now, but I still have to do a lot of soul-wrestling (Jordan, 1999) with it. This process of getting to know that shadow has become an important part of my own inner growth journey.

Pay special attention to the rests, the pauses, in a selection of music. These rests, where the music is silent, are important to the rhythm of the music. Can you imagine music without pauses? The times when there's no sound give you space to feel the music. This is a good analogy to life where the quiet moments—the rests—in your day are essential for the rhythm and the harmony of the whole.

3. Experiment with what works best for you.

   - Maybe you respond best to drums; rhythm instruments turn you on. Let the vibrations fill your body and soul. They can take you to some powerful inner places, as has been shown in studies of shamanism. Rhythm instruments have also been used successfully in music therapy.
   - Find out what kind of melodies you like and how they affect you. I always cry when I hear the simple folk songs of my childhood, especially when there's an accordion in the background.
   - If you have access to a piano, a guitar, or another instrument, maybe you want to take lessons. Guitar is fairly easy to learn if you just want to entertain yourself and your friends.
   - If you don't want to take time for formal lessons, just play around on an instrument, such as a guitar and piano. It's easy to create a melody and harmony on the strings and the piano keys.
   - Buy a harmonica! Just blowing in and out will create a harmony without much additional instruction. It's a fun instrument and easy to play. Buy a harmonica for your children or grandchildren.
   - Sing a song. Singing creates a habit of moving inner feelings to outside of you. Sing in the shower to join with the sound of the water.
   - Have you ever written a song? Maybe you should try it. Or you can write the lyrics and have someone set them to music. Sounds like what you did in college when you thought you were going to be a famous songwriter? Now you can write it just for yourself and forget the fame!
   - Be playful with music—whether listening, understanding, or performing.

- Try to translate your mood into a musical sound. Banging on a drum has been shown to help release tension (Lewis, 2004).
- Learn how you react to different kinds of music. How do dissonant sounds affect you? What kind of music relaxes and soothes you? What helps you concentrate? What energizes you?
- Music is also something you can easily do with a group. Nonprofessional group singing is almost a lost art, but you can try it, maybe at a holiday event. As a professor, the last class of the semester usually includes singing—and I play guitar, harmonica, and bells on my ankles all at the same time! My students have told me if I did this in their first class, they would have a different first impression of their professor.

WRITING

What Kind of Writing?

When asked what kind of writing they use for their Personal Growth, the administrators in my surveys listed the following types: personal and family letters, e-mail, journals, reflections, letters to editors, articles, and poems.

Do you keep a journal? Progoff (1992) has written an excellent research-based work that has become a classic on journal writing. His process is intended to enable the reader toward personal renewal, using the reality of outer experiences to work at the inner levels of life. His intensive journal method assists readers to "access the power of their unconscious" and to "develop interior capacities strong enough to be relied upon in meeting the trials of our life" (p. 18). Versluis (2004) describes a practice, previously referred to in chapter 6, that was used in the seventeenth and eighteenth centuries, the commonplace book. It was kept in a common place, such as a library. Anyone could come by and write down ideas, observations, thoughts, and insights into this book. The author advocates such contemplative writing as a way to "develop our inner awareness by bringing what we have experienced beyond ourselves and shaping it" (p. 61).

Do you want to write more just for yourself? Try reading Natalie Goldberg and Judith Guest's wonderful, humorous, and easy-to-read book, *Writing Down the Bones: Freeing the Writer Within* (1986), or one of Goldberg's many other works on creative writing. With her witty approach, Goldberg inspires would-be writers to take the leap into writing by offering suggestions, encouragement, and advice. You may find her ideas helpful even for the professional writing you have to do as an administrator.

Writing is a creative activity, but much more.
Writing is . . .

- an important tool for self-expression
- a vehicle for inner growth
- a way to clarify thoughts and feelings
- a record of where you've been and where you want to go
- a private getaway
- a means to link mind, body, and soul
- a journey into your inner landscape
- an opportunity to create peace by emptying your mind onto paper
- a place to record your dreams
- a means of communicating with yourself and others

Writing for your Personal Growth

As the above list indicates, writing has the potential to help you keep a balance in your life. Even though the focus here has been on reflective writing, some of this is also true about your professional writing. For example, writing helps you to clarify your thoughts and put them into some order. Writing by its nature slows you down. You can use it as a way to express your feelings about a situation before you take action. For example, when you are angry at someone, write an angry letter to that person— but don't mail it! When you get ready to confront that person or situation, your anger has already found an outlet and you will be more centered and calm in your reply.

Writing letters is a special kind of writing. Personally, I hope that the increasing use of electronic mail will not cause the demise of the art of writing letters; undoubtedly, e-mail will create its own genre of writing. A handwritten letter says that you took extra time and effort for someone. There are many examples in literature of letters written by someone that give advice, support, love, and empathy. For example, the poet Rainer Maria Rilke (1993) wrote a series of remarkable letters, from 1903–1908, to a young would-be poet on surviving as a sensitive observer in a harsh world. You can get to know yourself through the letters you write to others, and others will benefit from knowing more about you.

For writing to have an impact, as with all the Personal Growth practices, you must do it. Taking time is again a key issue. However, since writing a few lines doesn't take as much time, and since you can catch time for it in between other activities, it may be an easier habit to develop.

REFLECTIONS AND EXERCISES

1. Pay attention to your creative energy in everyday life. Cultivate curiosity and interest, a sense of wonder and awe. Here are some ways you can do this:

   > Set aside some time at the end of the day to reflect on something that surprised you that day.

   > Put creative energy into some routine activity in your daily schedule—do it differently and feel how it renews your excitement about it.

   > Change something in your space—your office, home environment, or, on a macro level, take a trip to a different place.

2. Internalize looking at things differently. Find a new way to express what moves you. If you are basically an introvert, try showing what you feel with an outer reaction—talk about it, or try smiling or crying. If you are an extrovert, try keeping your reactions inside and work through them by yourself—writing in a journal helps for this.

3. Find the spaces in-between. For a few days, become aware of how you filled the times in-between or during your routine activities. Here is an example: Where was your mind when you brushed your teeth or took a shower this morning, or when you were walking out to your car? Were you thinking about what you had to do that day? Did you fill those moments with intentional mindful breathing? Did you imagine the water washing off your soul and refreshing your spirit as you showered? Were you conscious of the crisp morning air as you walked outside?

4. Become more aware of beauty in everything.

5. Use all of your five senses to notice what is around you. Stop for just a few seconds and let what is beautiful about it enter your awareness. Keep a list somewhere of your discoveries:

   > the design of a building

   > the drawing of a child

   > the crooked limb of a tree

   > a fall leaf

   > the color of a flower

   > the smile of a friend

the light of the moon on the water

a moving face in the clouds

the feel of rain on your skin

6. Schedule a time when you will create a product: Paint something, draw something, try "doodling" in a meeting, make something from scraps, knit, sew, decorate—then accept your product without judging it or allowing anyone else to do so.

7. When you play or sing or listen to music, become aware of how you are using your global, intuitive, and emotional side (right-brain function). Then perceive how your logical, orderly, and analytical side (left-brain function) manifests itself. Note which is dominant in you and consciously practice developing the other side.

8. If you do not have a journal for your reflections, I'd urge you to purchase one—or develop a file in your computer for your reflections. If you already keep a journal, think about ways you could make it more beneficial to your Personal Growth.

8 Time for and With Yourself: Silence, Solitude, and Meditation

Be still and know that I am God . . .
Be still and know that I am . . .
Be still and know . . .
Be still . . .
Be . . .

—Psalm 46:10

DIFFICULT BUT CRUCIAL

Perhaps you're smiling at the title of this chapter. You can't imagine yourself meditating on company time? Maybe in the restroom? Where else do you have quiet and alone time? Yes, I know. For a busy administrator, this may be the most difficult of all practices, and certainly one of the most important. It is only in quiet times that serious reflection can take place. It is in times when you are alone that you can work on facing that inner garden, the real you, the part that gets covered over in your hectic daily life.

This chapter will discuss some similarities and differences among three activities: times of being alone (solitude), times of silence, and meditation. The exercises will help you learn how to use such times for your

Personal Growth. Some definitions, practices, and steps for meditation are included. Meditation is a natural and deeper extension of your quiet times. As you probably already know, practicing meditation has been proven to benefit the body as well as one's mental and spiritual health.

As for all Personal Growth practices, making time will be your biggest challenge. The good news is that you can learn to incorporate many of the practices in this chapter into your daily routines on an informal basis.

BEING IN THE PRESENT

What silence, solitude, and meditation have in common is a focus on the present moment, the now. Many books have been written about the importance of living in the moment, for example, the recent national best seller *The Power of Now* (Tolle, 1999), or a classic work of a few years ago, another best seller, *Wherever You Go There You Are* (Kabat-Zinn, 1994). You might want to purchase these two books or one of those listed below.

Here is one book that would be ideal for reading one page a day: *Everyday Serenity: Meditations for People Who Do Too Much* (Kundtz, 2000). Vietnamese Buddhist monk Thich Nhat Hanh, who was nominated for a Nobel Peace prize a few years ago, wrote a manual on meditation entitled *The Miracle of Mindfulness* (1976). Another one of his books, *Being Peace* (1987), includes a section on meditations in daily life. Medical doctor Jeffrey Brantley (2003) recommends mindfulness meditations for anxiety, fear, and panic in his book, *Calming Your Anxious Mind*.

This moment is all we have to work with. We need to develop a habit of being aware and mindful of whatever we are doing right now. Become aware right now of what you are thinking and feeling, of what is going on around you and inside you. Practice such moments of mindful awareness whenever you remember to do so. It is in such moments that we face our inner selves and learn who we are and who we want to be.

Versluis (2004) talks about a conspiracy of modern devices in our technological society that keep us from silence or solitude:

> I often think that the purpose of much that we have invented and produced is precisely to keep us from having to face ourselves or to be alone: every moment we can fill with noise and diversions is a moment we have escaped having to consider who we are and where, or worst of all, why we do what we do. (p. 88)

THE MIND AND HEART OF ADMINISTRATORS

Ardeth was my favorite superintendent when I was a principal. I later became her assistant superintendent and she became a dear mentor to me. One of her many wonderful qualities was her ability to be a good listener. What made her so? I always felt that she was completely present to me. She looked at me directly and didn't interrupt as I spouted forth whatever I had to say. Now I realize that she showed immense patience not to allow her mind to go racing ahead to where she already knew the solution would lie. She became a model for me, though I still have to watch that my mind isn't comparing, judging, and analyzing while I'm trying to listen to someone in the present moment.

I have practiced meditation for many years now and am getting better at giving my attention fully to this moment. I think it's especially difficult for school administrators to be completely present to other persons while being aware of their own feelings, thoughts, and insights. We are always caught up in solving problems, continuously paying attention to other people, to problems, issues, concerns, and to everyday routines. Throughout the day I try to be aware to take time to reflect and to be mindful of each encounter or activity.

When my graduate administrative students do their first shadow experience of an administrator, their major observation is always the same, "S/he never stops!" How, in such an existence, can you possible find, or build in, times of silence and being alone where you can reflect on your practice, on your thoughts, on your feelings?

The first step, as with anything, is to be aware that you need such times, that you need to be in touch with yourself inside, not just engage in thinking, seeing, and doing but to actually feel the present moment completely—with your inner and outer senses. According to Kabat-Zinn (1994), mindfulness has to do above all with attention and awareness. Only in this way can the busy administrator be fully present to those many others who look to him for leadership.

TIMES OF SILENCE

A few years ago, when I was a school district superintendent, I read a book while vacationing in Germany. I especially enjoyed reading it in my native language. The title intrigued me: *Ich hoerte auf die Stille* ("I listened to the silence"). It is the story of a Catholic priest, Henri Nouwen (1976), who spent 7 months in a Trappist monastery in complete silence. I could identify with his experiences of surprise, frustration, even annoyance. In my many years as a school administrator, being in silence had not been something with which I was very familiar. This book was just what I needed. It became the beginning of my own journey into my inner world, where I learned to become more reflective and to discover my true self.

You learn to practice silent awareness throughout your workday, even when you are surrounded by people. Finding moments of quiet wherever you are will help you develop a habit to be more aware of being in the present moment at all times. Even if you are in a crowded auditorium, on the playground, or in your own office, you can take a deep breath and spend a few seconds not saying a word. Just listen and be aware of what is going on around you and inside you.

Exercise for Silence: Find a place that is as quiet as possible and with the fewest probable distractions. It could be inside a building or outside, somewhere in nature. You can walk or sit in silence and become aware of your surroundings. You can do this exercise on your way from your office to a classroom, or to the playground. Allow all of your senses to be in touch with what is around you. Look and listen. Breathe deeply and become aware of the smells around you. Touch something near you—the bark of a tree, a flower petal, or a window pane. Become aware of, and try to use, all of your senses for this experience. Afterwards, you may want to write down what you heard in the silence and what your senses were receiving.

If you live in a city, you'll probably hear car noises from a freeway nearby. Sometimes when I close my eyes, I can easily pretend that they sound like ocean waves. In places outside of the city, in nature, there are also sounds in the silence. In these moments of listening to the silence, you will learn to become more aware of what is around you, and your reactions to it. You will also learn to be more aware and hear the sounds, the voices, coming from deep inside you. Just be open and listen and be with whatever you experience.

SOLITUDE: TIME TO BE ALONE

In solitude we give passionate attention to our lives, to our memories, to the details around us.

—Virginia Woolf

Seeking solitude, being alone somewhere, is one of the most difficult things to do for a busy school leader, or for any modern person today. When I was a child, my sister and I used to visit a castle in southern Germany named Solitude. It was nestled in a forest with walking paths and a park around it. Most of us probably don't have a real castle to go to, but it is important to create or find your own place of solitude.

How do you get away by yourself? Maybe you go for a drive and then park for a while looking over the ocean or at a mountain. Or you may sit in your favorite chair just looking out at your garden. Maybe you can learn to just be alone and centered within yourself, even in a crowded room. What happens when you are conscious of being alone?

Exercises for Solitude: Go somewhere to be alone. If it's a weekend, it might be in a building, such as a church or temple. A garden is a good place, or a park, the beach, or a rocky ledge on a mountain. Even if there are other people around, focus on the aloneness you feel and just be with yourself. Be aware of feelings, thoughts, and images, but don't get involved with them. You may want to bring your journal and make notes.

During your workday, close your office door for a few seconds or minutes. It might be especially useful just before you meet with an angry parent or face a difficult personnel conference. Sit physically still and close your eyes, even if just for a few seconds. Become aware of what thoughts come into your mind. What feelings arise? What do your inner voices tell you—insights, fears, conflicts—what is important to you right then? Then let those inner voices dissolve and find your center. Stay in that inner calm place as you go on to the next event in your workday or life.

Catch Your Breath

This simple, often-used phrase has an important truth: One of the ways you can always find a moment of being silent and centered within yourself, of being present in the moment, is to focus on your breathing. Many teachers of meditation, yoga, and other spiritual practices mention the importance of breathing. There are specific exercises for breathing which you may want to look up in one of the books on meditation that I have listed. Your breath is something that is always with you, and can be used at any time to focus on the present moment.

You can use an awareness of your breathing as a pause, a break, a time-out, a stillpoint (Kundtz, 2000) in between your constant flow of activities. I would urge you to develop a habit of being aware of your breathing in whatever you do. If you forget (and you will), the very moment that you become aware of how you're breathing, stop and consciously breathe more deeply and calmly. When you're in a stressful situation, you will probably find your breathing to be shallow and fast. Consciously take a deep breath and feel it fill your body. Then, as you breathe out, mentally let go of whatever anxiety you may be experiencing. Repeat this three or four times while focusing on the center of your body, watching your in and out breaths.

Focusing on your breathing is also useful to fill the transitions between your activities throughout the day. It is a simple way to create pauses of stillness and calm wherever you are. Your breath is always with you. You might also try this at night when your mind is racing up and down your to-do list, and won't let your body go to sleep. Counting your in and out breaths helps to let go of the thoughts, and will almost always help you get that sleep and rest you desire.

Knowing Yourself Through Silence and Solitude

"Why is it important to seek times of silence and being alone?" you might ask. The English novelist Aldous Huxley said, "Silence is full of potential wisdom and wit as the unhewn marble of great sculpture." Not a bad metaphor for educators, who must discover the potential of young people and form their lives as a sculptor molds his masterpiece from an undeveloped block of raw material! Wisdom doesn't come easily. Times for reflection, silence, and time alone are necessary so that you can help your mind and your heart absorb insights, sort out impressions, and gain the wisdom from experiences that tumble through you at such a fast rate all day long.

I like how Thomas Merton (1958) defined solitude as not necessarily traveling from one geographical possibility to another. He states that a person becomes a solitary "at the moment when, no matter what may be his external surroundings, he is suddenly aware of his own inalienable solitude and sees that he will never be anything but solitary" (p. 81). According to Merton, we are essentially alone even in the midst of a busy world.

One way to be in solitude is to learn to turn inward and become aware of our inner solitary world. Susuki (1996) advocates a beginner's mind that is still and open, asking what it is doing now, what it is thinking now, seeing things as always fresh and new. In the chapter called "The Almond Tree in Your Front Yard," Thich Nhat Hanh (1976) illustrates the supreme importance of mindfulness in everything we do. Looking at the tree with an open heart and experiencing it as a wonder of reality will help us to see all beings with eyes of compassion.

MEDITATION: A USEFUL AND HEALTHY PRACTICE

More and more corporations are encouraging their employees to take time during the workday for formal or informal meditation. Some companies have created special places and times for their executives to learn and practice meditation. They understand that times spent in silence and reflection will lead to better mental and physical health of their employees, as well as better decision-making for their leaders.

Maybe you're thinking that you don't want your staff to see you meditate, since most school systems don't yet have an executive workout or time-out room. But the benefits of some kind of meditation practice are so great that you will want to incorporate into your life both formal and informal periods of meditation.

The August 30, 2004, issue of *Business Week* carried an article by Michelle Conlin (2004) entitled "Meditation: New Research Shows That It Changes the Brain in Ways That Alleviate Stress." The article describes research done at the National Institutes of Health as well as several universities to document how meditation enhances the qualities companies need in their human capital: sharpened intuition, steely concentration, and plummeting stress levels. The author discusses several types of meditations and concludes with this humorous antidote for our busy lives, "The point is: Don't just do something—sit there" (p. 137).

Meditating is not something foreign, something done as part of the New Age movement. Formal meditation has been practiced by numerous religious and spiritual traditions, particularly in the Eastern world, as a way to get in touch with oneself and/or a higher being for thousands of years. Since the 1960s, the Western world has become more interested in meditation, especially as it relates to health and well-being.

In relating the benefits of a meditation practice to gain freedom from anxiety, fear, and panic, Brantley (2003) talks about meditation as being a turning inward to discover our capacity for calm, steadiness, and awareness. His approach is to develop mindfulness, which he defines as a friendly, nonjudging, present-moment awareness. He believes that mindfulness is developed through a daily practice of meditation.

The purpose of meditation is not a special kind of enlightenment, but, as Peter Matthiessen states in *The Snow Leopard* (Kabat-Zinn, 1994), it is a way to "pay attention even at unextraordinary times, to be of the present, nothing-but-the-present, to bear this mindfulness of now into each event of ordinary life" (p. 200).

Being in silence and alone is a natural bridge to meditating. Meditation is a way to deepen our attention and awareness and put it to greater practical use in our daily lives. When you are alert and listening to sounds around and within you, including your own thoughts and feelings, you create a special state of awareness. This is exactly what you do when you meditate. A major difference is that in meditation, your thoughts and external stimuli play a different role. In meditation you learn to listen to, and be in touch with, your inner self.

What Is Meditation?

There are many types of meditation from the Eastern traditions as well as meditations practiced by Western spiritual and religious groups. Meditation is also increasingly being used by medical professionals as an aid for mind and body healing. Meditation might be used in the sense of meditating on something, such as a memory or a selection from a spiritual reading; or reflecting on a work of art, or perhaps a dream image. In a broad sense, meditation includes discursive thinking and reasoning, as well as what Christians call contemplation, Hindus call *samadhi,* and Buddhists call Zen.

Johnson (1997) defines meditation simply as the search for wisdom. Levine (1989) calls meditation awareness and advocates that we directly participate in each moment as it occurs with as much awareness and understanding as possible. A great little book to help you get started with meditation is by Anderton (2003), who defines meditation as the creation of a relaxed state of awareness of mind and body (p. 12). Scientist and spiritual writer Gary Zukav (1979) states, "Do not be surprised if physics curricula in the twenty-first century include classes in meditation" (p. 327).

The basic difference among various forms of meditation is that each uses a different primary object of awareness on which to concentrate. For Sufis, it may be dancing; in Zen, chanting mantra or sitting meditations; for Christians (Keating, 1997), a contemplative centering prayer. Objects of concentration may include an inner mental or visual image, an external object (e.g., a flower, a mandala, or a religious icon), repeating a word or phrase (sometimes called a mantra), an inspirational piece of music, or just being mindful of your breathing. In mindfulness meditation approaches, taught in the Buddhist traditions, the object of concentration is merely to pay attention in a way so as to be more aware, without judgment, of the present moment, and all that is here now.

What all meditative practices have in common is the idea of bringing our attention to a deeper, inner level of experience, rather than staying with the rational mind with its continuous stream of thoughts commenting, judging, and planning. Through meditation, we learn to get in touch with all parts of ourselves, including those aspects that are blocked, hidden, or unconscious in our everyday life of thinking and mind action. The true nature of our being lies much deeper—and meditation opens us to this level of consciousness where we learn who we really are. We are more than our thoughts; we are more than our feelings or emotions. By learning to live in the Now (Tolle, 1999), we become completely present to the situation at hand, and can draw on the wisdom from our whole self, using all of the inner resources at our disposal to respond appropriately in that moment.

The practical and physical benefits of meditation have been well recognized and documented. Some kind of a practice of meditation is an important part of your Personal Growth because it opens a path to your inner self. Meditation has the potential to lead you to deeper self-knowledge, to a more relaxed daily life, a clearer perspective, and better appreciation of the connectedness of all life.

Most leaders have learned to be good at intellectual decision-making. We can break down a problem situation into steps, and even apply some research-based theories to come up with a rational solution. But what about decisions of the heart, where emotions are involved? Many of us are not as good with these. When faced with moral dilemmas in our workplace, we are sometimes unsure of the best alternatives because we rely primarily on that well-functioning and well-trained machine of our intellectual mind. Meditation is one way to address the stress created when there's a conflict between a *should* and a *want* in our decisions, as we discussed in the first chapter. During the past 10 years, my daily practice of meditation has helped me to know myself and to make better choices for myself, as well as in my relationships with others.

A Formal Meditation Practice

"So," you ask, "what does this mean to me? You've convinced me that I need to begin meditating, but how do I start? What do I do?"

Most importantly, you need to set aside some time. I know that's difficult, but begin with just a few minutes a day. For me, it's the first thing in the morning. Try setting your alarm just a few minutes earlier. Begin with five minutes and gradually increase your meditation to 20 minutes a day. Once you develop a habit of this, it will get easier and you will miss not doing it, just as you would not think of leaving the house without brushing your teeth. An important benefit of such a daily formal meditation practice is that you will find it easier to be in a reflective/meditative mode throughout your busy days.

After teaching meditation for several years, I have developed some simple steps that I believe will help you get started. I would also encourage you to invest in some of the books listed in this chapter to learn more about meditation practices. I have included three practices below that demonstrate various ways to meditate. The first one is a simple visualization, the second uses a word or phrase, and the last combines these two. For those of you wanting to try more meditations, I have included an additional one in the Resource notes for this chapter.

Suggested Process for Meditation

1. *Be still:* Create a quiet, sacred space that you can call your meditation place. I have used a special chair in a corner of my home looking out

onto a tree. Next to it, I have placed some objects, a candle, and some stones and feathers that I have collected as well as some other symbols that remind me of what is important in my life. Sit comfortably in a relaxed position. Use a straight back chair and place your feet flat on the floor, unless you prefer a lotus position (legs crossed sitting on a pillow). Cup your hands one into the other. Slightly tilt your head forward and, if you want to, close your eyes. Now become aware of your breathing. You may want to mentally repeat something with your in and out breath: "breathing in, breathing out," or "peace in, peace out." Now slowly take an inventory of the physical sensations of your body, the energy flow, the movements you feel inside you and on your skin. Do this with all parts of your body, beginning with your feet, up through the torso, your head, arms, and then rest your attention on the region of your heart. This will help you to be completely present in your body and in this moment.

2. *Select your focus:* This may be a mental or external visual image, a sound, a word, or phrase (mantra)—perhaps something from a spiritual reading. Place your attention in a place in your body—I recommend the region of your heart, but in Eastern traditions the center of the forehead is sometimes used. Focus your attention on that place in your body while maintaining your awareness on the object (visual image or word) you have chosen. Close your eyes and maintain this focused awareness throughout your meditation time. Open your eyes briefly when you need to reestablish the connection if you are using an external object.

3. *Have a spiritual intention:* Although it is not the purpose of meditation to be enlightened, your desire is to gain wisdom, meaning, knowledge of yourself, to get in touch with the part of you that you call spiritual. It is your choice as to what you want to call it, such as the divine within you, your higher power, God, universal spirit, your true self, the highest good, or whatever you prefer, based on your own spiritual or religious tradition. Maintain this desire and intention even when thoughts intrude—and they will. Be careful not to seek too strongly or with too much goal orientation. It is more a quiet and yielding desire, an opening up to the spirit inside you. Thich Nhat Hanh's (1976) recommendation for beginners is the "method of pure recognition: recognition without judgment" (p. 61).

4. *Let thoughts go by:* Thoughts include perceptions, feelings, images, memories, reflections, and mental commentaries. Remember that your meditation is a time to allow a deeper part of yourself to be in control. You can get back to your conscious thoughts at a later time. Your meditation time will help you to learn that thoughts, especially your intellectual mind, are not all that matter. This will carry over into your daily life, so that you can become more aware and learn to let go, for example, of

anxious thoughts, worries, or frivolous thoughts and negative feelings. You will gradually become more conscious of what is truly important, of the inner wisdom of your whole being.

Letting go of thoughts does not mean that you are to deny your thoughts and feelings. They are real and a part of you and need to be expressed, acknowledged, and worked through. But your meditation time is not when you want to do this. In meditation you just acknowledge your thoughts and feelings, are aware of them, and then allow them to pass by—like clouds floating by a mountain. You may use one of your times of silence and solitude, as described above, to do inner work on the thoughts and feelings that keep coming up from within you (see Robert Johnson's *Inner Work*, 1986).

5. *Trust:* All will be well. Surrender, accept, and know that a power within you is at work to help you be the best you can be, and that your life does have meaning. With time and practice, it will become easier for you to center and focus more quickly on your inner place so that you can let go of anxieties and stress, and make wiser decisions in your everyday life.

Three Meditations to Practice

Meditation Practice # 1: Visualization

One of the simplest ways to practice meditation is to use your imagination and visualize yourself in a place that is safe and peaceful for you. For some, this is a place in nature, or inside a comfortable room with a window looking out. You may use a visual image from a past experience, a piece of art, or a scene from a spiritual book. As you sit in your imagination, be aware and focus on your surroundings; allow the peace and relaxation of that place to be with you, and in you. You may invite into your imaginary space another being to sit with you in your meditation.

For the busy administrator, if you don't have time to sit down or close your eyes during this visualization, you can learn to go to your pleasant image with your eyes open, and even in the midst of a crisis. This can become a way for you to gain a different perspective on an immediate situation and can help you to create a more peaceful mind. It may be helpful to be in your imaginary place as you are on your way to settle an argument, to negotiate an agreement, or to convince someone of a need in your school.

Meditation Practice # 2: Using a Word or Phrase (Mantra)

Using a word or short phrase and repeating it helps your mind to become silent. You might chose a verse from a sacred book, a simple prayer, a word for your deity, the name of a loved one, or a simple word like love, compassion, peace, or joy. Repeat this word or phrase until your heart becomes still. Use it again if you find your mind wandering. This exercise is also useful in everyday life to calm you when you find yourself getting anxious or stressed. Just repeat your word while focusing on your inner self so that you can reestablish your connection with inner peace.

Meditation Practice # 3: Combining Image and Words

An example of this type of meditation is described by an anonymous 14th-century author in a work entitled *The Cloud of Unknowing* (Wolters, 1978). It combines a visual image and the use of a word or phrase. For this one you will want to be in a quiet space and set aside some time.

Use the following mental image: As you sit in silence, imagine that you are sitting between two clouds—the Cloud of Unknowing above you, and the Cloud of Forgetting beneath you.

The Cloud of Unknowing symbolizes that you can never know through your intellect all of what's above you: your deity, your God, the mystery of life, the universe, even all of your Self. As you sit in your meditation, use a simple word or phrase and send it up to that cloud above you to show your desire to directly experience that mystery, the divine, and to get to know your true self.

The Cloud of Forgetting beneath you is to be used to place all of the thoughts and feelings—of the past, present, or future—that occur to you during your meditation. You sit in between the two clouds, unengaged in thoughts and with nothing but a desire to know and be known through love, through a direct experience of the divine, the mystery. Use your sacred word or phrase to maintain contact with the Cloud above you and place any thoughts or feelings that arise under the Cloud beneath you.

Informal Meditation

You can look for opportunities all day long to take a time-out for meditation and inner reflection. Allow yourself to be completely present in whatever is going on. Be aware of your thoughts, your feelings, of what is around you. You can sharpen your sense perception by consciously using all of your senses to be in the moment: Stand still for a second and look up at the clouds as you walk across your school campus. Listen to the sounds of children laughing, smell the rain enlivening the dry soil, taste each bite of your food with mindfulness, touch the leaf of a tree.

Be aware of your thoughts without judging them. Maybe you notice that you are experiencing anxious thoughts about your next appointment. Brantley (2003) emphasized the importance of practicing compassion and kindness for yourself (and others) as you pay attention and practice awareness.

Do It Anyway

If you have tried some of the meditations in this chapter, and have sat in silence, if you even have begun to do this on a regular basis—developing it as a habit, as part of your daily life—you are to be commended! However, if you're not experiencing results right away—whatever you want these to be for you—don't stop! In fact, don't meditate to achieve some purpose. A formal meditation practice is a spiritual discipline and something that needs to be practiced until it becomes a habit, a part of your routine.

The effects are not always immediately apparent, though for you they may be. For me, with my history of a skeptical and rational mind orientation, it has taken a long time, and I've often not felt anything special during my meditations. Some people report that they have, for example, experienced some higher level of consciousness, perhaps being surrounded or filled with light or warmth. Perhaps you will have such enlightenment experiences during your meditation practice, but enlightenment is not the purpose of meditation.

Meditating and centering in silence is something you do because you know that it is crucial to your inner Personal Growth, as well as your physical health (although meditation is not primarily a relaxation technique). You can't see a plant growing, but you know that it is. When other people tell you that you've become a bit more patient or show less agitation in certain situations, you'll know that it's related to whatever has been happening deep inside in those times that you've dedicated to your inner self. And it's guaranteed to make a difference in the long run by helping you to connect with all the parts of yourself, to be in better balance, and to know who you are, and who you want to be in your life.

REFLECTIONS AND EXERCISES

Ask yourself these questions. Write your reflections in your journal.

1. When, today (or this week), did I give myself the gift to be alone for a while? What did I experience during these moments?

2. In each situation today—when I had to make a decision, perform a task, talk with someone, solve a problem—was I able to be completely present and use all of my senses to be aware of what was

happening around and within me? How did I show that I was present to the other person?

3. When did I feel centered today, able to draw on my inner wisdom, calm and peaceful in the knowledge that I would know what to do? How did I react? How did the other person react?

4. When did I not feel centered today, but felt conflicted, agitated, rushed, stressed, angry, disappointed, hurt, impatient, rejected, anxious? What did I do with these feelings—deny them, forgive myself, forgive others, explode, raise my voice, lose my cool, count to ten or bite my tongue, redirect them, visualize a positive image, mentally repeat a word, have compassion, do an affirmation, send someone away? What was the impact on others?

5. Have I taken time today (or this week) to get to know myself, to develop myself in the spiritual dimensions of my being? What times and places seem to work best for me to get away and renew myself?

6. How am I establishing a formal meditation practice? Do I have a special space set aside in my home for this purpose? Do I have a time set aside? What seems to be my best time of the day?

9 Dreamwork: Knowing Your Whole Self

If one advances confidently in the direction of his dreams, and endeavors to live a life which he has imagined, he will meet with a success unexpected in common hours.

—Henry David Thoreau

WHAT DO YOU MEAN BY DREAMS?

When the surveys came back from my studies of administrators, it immediately became clear to me that the term *dreams* didn't mean to the participants what I had intended it to mean. I was thinking of working on dreams occurring during our nightly sleep. However, most of the participating administrators seemed to equate it with dreams of achievement, or dreams and hopes for something in the future—as in the phrases "May your dreams come true" or "Follow your dreams."

Here are examples of comments made by the respondents: "I often stop to reflect on what works and what would or could be improved." "I do this about work and projects at home." Even though these comments didn't match what I originally had in mind, and dreams was ranked as the least used practice, these comments made me realize that there really were two types of dreams that could contribute to our Personal Growth. So I'm calling one type *day dreams* and the other *night dreams*.

DAY DREAMS: YOUR THOUGHTS HAVE POWER

When I began to look around for examples of the kind of dreams these administrators talked about, I found a surprising number of them. Do you remember the baseball movie called *Field of Dreams* from a few years ago? An inspirational writer, Mary M. Morrissey (1996) entitled her book *Building Your Field of Dreams*. She introduces her work with these words: "Whoever you are, whatever your background, wherever you are in your journey . . . I invite you to discover a way of living that will make the dreams of your heart come true" (p. xi). She outlines certain spiritual principles that can turn such dreams into reality.

The title of the autobiography and journals by Helen Luke (2000), a remarkable woman, a Jungian analyst who studied with C. G. Jung himself, was *Such Stuff as Dreams Are Made On*. She includes both types of dreams by weaving together dreams and symbolic images from her inner life with personal and world events.

Bestselling author Deepak Chopra (1994), in his book entitled *The Seven Spiritual Laws of Success: A Practical Guide to the Fulfillment of Your Dreams*, includes a beautiful quote from the ancient Upanishad scriptures that is pertinent to this topic:

- You are what your deep, driving desire is.
- As your desire is, so is your will.
- As your will is, so is your deed.
- As your deed is, so is your destiny. (inside cover page)

Everyone is familiar with Martin Luther King's classic "I Have a Dream" speech. In four short paragraphs he describes his longing for that day when his dream will come true.

Let's talk a bit about day dreams. I don't mean "day dreams" in the sense of unachievable ideals like soap bubbles that quickly burst, but dreams as goals, as ideas that can be fulfilled. Psychologists, philosophers, spiritual, and religious teachers tell us that all human beings have a dream for doing something out of the ordinary, something special with their lives.

A recent study of principals was conducted by Robert Vouga (2003) entitled, "Why do Effective Administrators Choose to Remain in 'the Hot Seat?'" Vouga found that the greatest source of satisfaction—and the most important reason why principals stayed in their jobs—was that they wanted to "help children learn, help teachers increase their effectiveness, help people solve problems and effect change" (p. 72). That's a worthwhile dream, isn't it?

What is your dream for your work? What kind of leader do you dream of being? What about your personal dreams? Have you always wanted to play an instrument, go to Europe, write a book, get a doctorate, live on a ranch? What changes are you willing to make that will help you fulfill these dreams? Maybe you can't make all of them come true, and not all at once, but you can gradually move toward some of them.

Here is something emphasized in many of the self-help books. If you believe something in your heart and truly desire it, you can let your mind in on it by repeating positive affirmations on this desire, this dream. This will help you to move toward its achievement. To make something a reality, you can begin by thinking about and reflecting on it. Your thoughts have power. Your mind, once it believes something is possible, will help you formulate a plan to get there.

A DREAM COME TRUE

One of my role models for achieving her dreams is Mary. Mary was an eighth grade student in the school where I was a principal. She was a troubled teenager from a broken home. She ran away at 16 and joined the air force. At 18, she married and had three children. Mary never graduated from high school and, after leaving the military, worked at McDonald's hamburgers to help support herself and her family. She got a disability check to help make ends meet. The marriage didn't work out. Sounds like a familiar scenario so far? Well, here is the surprise way Mary made her own dreams come true. And in the process, she also made one of my dreams come true.

Mary called me one evening about 5 years after I knew her as an eighth grader. She told me she had just named her first child after me! I was so excited, I didn't even ask for her address. Ten years later, Christa, my namesake, began writing to me, and we've corresponded ever since. I went to Christa's high school graduation in Oregon and to her college graduation from a prestigious private institution. Christa was a smart girl. She had applied for so many scholarships and loans to a college that she had dreamed of going to, that it actually cost her less to attend there than it would have cost her to attend a state school. Christa is now working on her master's degree and I hope to attend her wedding sometime soon.

Mary is proud of her Christa. Her own dreams to finish school and to make something of her life may have fallen short of her expectations—though she's actually working on them now—but she has realized some of her dreams through her daughter. And my dream of having a child became a reality because Christa has become like a daughter to me. Young

Christa is working to achieve her own life's dreams. She is a determined and wonderful young woman who knows very much what she wants. Mary and I are both very proud of her. This very personal story also illustrates the importance of taking one small step toward your dreams. For Mary and for me it was the naming of a little baby girl.

NIGHT DREAMS: YES YOU DO HAVE THEM!

This is what I really wanted to talk about when I sent out my surveys: using the dreams you have during sleep to help with Personal Growth. How many of you keep track of any of your nightly dreams? My husband swears he never dreams, but there is scientific evidence to the contrary. We all dream. In fact, research has shown that even animals dream. Hall (1966), as director of the Institute of Dream Research, did some early research on rapid eye movement (REM) periods, when dreaming apparently takes place. He found that when cats were deprived of REM sleep, they became psychotic. Thus, it seems that dreaming is important, and even good for you.

REMEMBERING YOUR DREAMS

Do you remember your dreams? Here are some suggestions for learning to recall your dreams. Keep a notebook by your bedside. Train yourself (this will take some practice) whenever you wake up—in the mornings or in the middle of the night—to immediately ask, "What did I dream?" Then, in a half-asleep state, with your eyes still closed, go back into the dream images and try to resurrect the key elements as quickly as possible. Then write down the scene, the characters, the feelings, and the events of the dream. Write the main ones first, then fill in the details later. Don't worry if what you write at that time doesn't appear to be logical or sequential, or even seem very special. The place from which dreams come, your unconscious, is quite a different kind of place, where anything is possible. You may only recall snatches of images, but it's a start to get you to work on remembering your dreams.

MESSAGES FROM YOUR INNER WORLD

Why should you remember your dreams? Because they will take you to a place, an inner land, that is not accessible to your conscious mind. Dreams can teach you a lot about what is going on in that inner world. Dreams are said to be messages from the unconscious. You dream a particular dream because your unconscious has your best interest at heart. It wants to reveal something to you that you need to know. That communication will help you gain important insights for what is going on in your life. Dreams give you a glimpse of an unbelievably rich inner landscape full of images and characters that are at your disposal if you learn how to access them.

How do I know this? Well, not only from personal experience, though I've kept track of my dreams for many years and have had professional help in analyzing them, but also because many psychologists and others have done a lot of research on dreams. There have been organizations and institutions established particularly for the study of dreams. There are numerous dream dictionaries that will interpret symbols from your dreams. Religious scriptures are full of stories about visions and dreams that helped set directions for action of the dreamers. We have learned about the importance of dreams from the great psychologists of the past century, Freud and Jung, and others. Their writings and the work of prac-titioners, particularly Jungian analysts, can help you interpret your dreams so that you can learn to apply them to becoming a more whole and well-functioning person (e.g., Johnson, 1986).

The depth to which you want to get into your dreams as a way for Personal Growth is completely up to you. In the following section, I will give you some basic guidelines that I have found useful, based on experi-ences, theories, and research.

How do dreams speak to us? Dreams use the language of symbols. You may want to purchase one of those dictionaries of dream symbols. I've included a couple of them in the references (Chevalier & Gheerbrant, 1996; Craze, 2004). One (Craze) was given to me by my students when they found out I loved studying dreams. It has beautiful photo illustrations that you might enjoy. The other (Chevalier & Gheerbrant) is a well-researched dictionary of symbols in general, which was originally published in 1969. You can find an increasing number of such dream interpretation books in any bookstore.

However, a word of caution when using such dream interpretation books: It's best to take all of their interpretations with a grain of salt. In other words, you are the only one who can really know what a particular image or symbol from your dream means to you. But it's fun to study them and, if nothing else, you can learn a lot about ancient civilizations, world religions, myths, and philosophies from such books.

Dreams also speak to us by showing us parts of ourselves that are unconscious. C. G. Jung calls these our personal shadow and archetypes from our collective unconscious. If you're interested in learning more about this, you might read Jung's classic, *Memories, Dreams, and Reflections* (Jaffe, 1989). Jungian analyst John Sanford (1989), in his book *Dreams: God's Forgotten Language,* discusses dreams and visions in the scriptures and emphasizes the inner reality of God as the source of our life and energies, as one who speaks through our dreams, our relationships, and the events of our life (p. 183). You might also want to learn more about what male and female characters may mean in your dreams by reading some of the books listed in the references.

DOING DREAMWORK: FOUR STEPS

Here are four steps to analyze and interpret your dreams that I have successfully used and taught to others in workshops. They are based mainly on the work of Robert Johnson (1986), a Jungian analyst, and are described in greater detail in his book, *Inner Work: Using Dreams and Active Imagination for Personal Growth.*

Step One: Associations

Write down all the characters and scenes you recall from a particular dream. Then take each one of these and write an association. Johnson (1986) defines association as any word, idea, mental picture, feeling, or memory that pops into your mind when you look at the image in the dream. What does each part of your dream remind you of? What comes to your mind? As stated before, use personal associations, rather than those from dream books or dictionaries of symbolism (unless you sense that they click with your own personal meaning).

Step Two: Connections

Connect with the events that are currently going on in your life. What is troubling you? What are you elated about? What are your real-life concerns, problems, or experiences that might be represented by the situation in the dream? What are the inner dynamics, the emotional events, conflict situations that you are experiencing right now? What traits do you have in common with the images or characters in the dream? What parts of you are the female dream characters or the masculine figures in your dream? Are there animals in your dream? What part of your own physical or instinctual energy systems might these represent? Write down the events in your life, and how you feel they might be symbolized by the dream images.

Step Three: Interpretation

In this step, you want to ask for the central, most important, message that this dream is trying to communicate to you. What is the dream trying to tell you? What is in the dream that is not a part of your conscious attitude? Is there something in your dream that you were not aware of in your mind, but that "rings a bell" with you? Remember that your dreams are about you! If your dream reflects an external situation, it will reveal something about your own attitudes and unconscious behavior patterns toward it. Live with the dream for a while and read your associations again. Return to the dream regularly so that your understanding of it increases. Then write as succinctly as possible what you think the central message of your dream might be. As you live with an important dream for the next few weeks, or even months and years, you may discover other messages as well.

Step Four: Ritual

This is the fun part! Doing a ritual requires that you do something, some physical act that will affirm the message of your dream. I often write a poem about a dream. Once I bought a yellow bag that I happened to see at a sidewalk sale after a dream I had soon after my mother died. I dreamed that I was bringing some gifts to her in a yellow bag. In my dream I was on a long and arduous journey, where I lost the bag and then found it again buried in a sandy cemetery. I didn't know what gifts were inside the bag, so the yellow bag I bought kept the search for its meaning alive for several years afterwards.

When I dream about taking walks in a green valley or a forest, I know it's time for me to take some time off. When I have a recurring dream (mine is usually about trying to catch a train and having too much luggage, or losing my bags), I pay particular attention. If your dream is telling you that you need more relaxation, make a ritual of taking yourself to a special place, perhaps out in nature. Johnson (1986) says that "doing a physical act has a magical effect on dream work" (p. 99). I would certainly agree with this from personal experience.

Writing down or painting a dream is a wonderful ritual. Sally Nelson (2004) wrote a fascinating and wonderful book on how to combine writing with dreaming. The key purpose of the ritual step is to remember your dream, to honor it, to make it concrete, and to let it live on for a while. Your dream will continue to speak to you each time you come in touch with the product of your ritual.

I hope you will get to know your inner landscape through your dreams and see what they might teach you. I guarantee that you will find it a challenging and exciting experience.

REFLECTIONS AND EXERCISES

1. Make a list of one or two "day dreams" you've had in the past. Take each and ask yourself the following questions:
   - When did this dream first begin?
   - What will it look like when it's finished, when it's been accomplished?
   - What have I done so far to work toward its fulfillment?
   - What steps will I take to make this dream a reality?

2. Begin a dream journal as suggested in this chapter. Don't get discouraged if you have trouble remembering all of a dream. Just write down the images, characters, and feelings you remember.

3. Take some dream that seems to be more clear than others (you can sense it is an "important" dream) and apply the four steps suggested in this chapter.

4. If you want to go into more depth, buy one of the books on dreams listed in the references.

10 Spending Time With Those Who Care About You: Another Way to Balance

In everyone's life, at some time, our inner fire goes out. It is then burst into flame by an encounter with another human being. We should all be thankful for those people who rekindle the inner spirit.

—Albert Schweitzer

In this chapter we will talk about another important way to renew yourself and to keep a balance in your life: spending time with others. In my first study of administrators, I had not included this element as one of the Personal Growth practices, because I was focusing mainly on what the administrator would do for and by himself. However, the responses from the participants were quite clear. They felt that spending time with others was indeed a very important way to relax and to renew. In the subsequent surveys, I added this as a choice and was not surprised that, along with physical activities, it was ranked at the top on the list of practices used for Personal Growth.

What types of activities did administrators do together with their families and friends? Here are the responses from the participants: travel; vacations; weekend trips; watching movies or television together; volunteer work; going to movies, plays, and concerts; recreation time; talking on the phone with long-distance friends; playing with grandchildren; visiting; playing cards; cooking, eating, drinking together; being with their spouse.

The following activities were placed in the "other" category on the surveys. These might also be called a kind of distraction or diversion activity. Many of them could also be done with family and friends. Here is the list of diversions that were mentioned: shopping, cultural events, visiting historical places, art galleries, sporting events, movies, grocery shopping, gardening and yard work, bookstores, sailing, car racing, cooking, fixing things, cleaning, watching television, filmmaking, playing bridge, home decorating, fishing, boating, home improvements, motorbiking, flying, drinking a glass of wine, smoking a cigar, going to a vacation home, and sports events. There is actually some research cited by Goleman (1995) that shows that such distraction activities may work well to lift one's moods during stressful times.

THE TRIAD OF BALANCE

In monasticism, particularly in the Benedictine tradition, there are three strands that are considered important for a monk to practice: *cloister*, or time in solitude; *community*, or time with other monks; and *hospitality*, time for opening up to those who are strangers (Homan & Pratt, 2002). These must be in a holistic balance in a monk's life.

For a school leader, a similar triad could be set up: time alone, time with friends, and time for causes. Let's look at three administrators and how each might represent these strands.

First, there is Hadley. He is a district administrator for special programs. He loves writing grants and is very good at it. He does wonderful charts in Excel and distributes them with his weekly memos to the principals. He writes clearly and is well respected for his expertise. But Hadley has one problem. He is basically a loner. He'd much rather do things sitting behind his computer, develop strategic plans and assessment documents, and then send them out to those who need to implement them. He has a hard time with the required meetings of leadership teams to get input on the operational aspects of his projects. He already knows what needs to be done, and he becomes very frustrated trying to listen to the group without telling them immediately what the decisions ought to be. "He's just not a people-person," his superintendent says, "but he's good with written work and technology."

Angel is gregarious, well-liked, everyone's mother. She's the principal of a large school. She's known as a workaholic, leaving school late and arriving early. Some feel she could manage her time better, but they love the attention she gives each person who crosses her path. She is interested in each of them and they trust her. Angel is the same with her large family on the weekends. She's a wonderful grandmother to her two grandchildren and spends most Saturdays taking them places or playing with them. She doesn't have children or a husband at home, so she often meets another principal friend at a restaurant after hours before she goes home. Only on Sundays does she spend the necessary time to do things for herself, such as shopping for groceries, doing laundry, or cleaning her house. She doesn't mind her lifestyle, though she sometimes wonders to herself, "Where does my time go?"

Toni is an activist. She's always been involved in various causes. As director of health and safety for her district, she attends community block meetings and listens to concerns of the neighborhood about the school and community. She is unafraid of the bureaucracies in her town when it comes to advocating for a change that would be good for the children. She gives of herself unselfishly and continuously. Everyone knows that if there's a problem to be solved, it's Toni who will jump in and assist. It was said that she even took in a homeless family once, and that she rode on the "nanny" bus from her inner city apartment to the suburbs and gave out her business card to everyone she met. Toni has a winning smile and immediately makes contact with strangers. She is a good listener and problem solver. "Her problem is that she has no personal life," a colleague admitted, "I hope she'll get a high reward in the next life."

Which of these three administrators is the most balanced? You are correct: None of them. A well-balanced leader needs time alone, in solitude, and time with others. Angel seems afraid of being with herself and escapes into her community of friends and family. Hadley is isolating himself from relationships. Although he is surrounded by people who need his attention, he keeps people at a distance. The sad thing is that he is also keeping life at a distance and may not be noticing what is going on with himself and his relationships with others. Toni, though well-intentioned, is spending all of her time and energy with those who she believes need her. She is missing the comforting and peaceful presence of good friends and family. She is probably also missing times of reflecting on her active, outwardly oriented life. Is she losing her inner self in the process?

WHY RELATE TO OTHERS?

Thomas Moore (1994) talks about relationships as being "truly sacred, not in the superficial meaning of simply being high in value, but in that they call upon infinite and mysterious depths in ourselves, in our communities, and in the very nature of things" (p. viii).

We learn from family and friends how we grow and who we are. They help us find our shadow. C. G. Jung (1960) talked about the importance of other people in one's process of individuation: "Individuation does not shut one out from the world, but gathers the world to oneself" ("Essay on the Nature of the Psyche," p. 226). Jung is credited with saying that anyone can go off to a mountaintop and be enlightened, but you need to go down to the marketplace and live it out among others. Jung also insisted that his closest personal students (disciples) not live alone, but live in a community with at least one other person.

We are unique individuals, but we are in a world with other people. We cannot help but interact with each other: Self and Other. In his five-point definition of emotional intelligence, Goleman (1995) includes the following two components that are related to relationships. To be emotionally intelligent means, among other things, the ability to

- Recognize emotions in others—empathy is a fundamental people skill
- Handle relationships—skill in managing the emotions of others (social competence)

The components of interpersonal intelligence listed by Goleman (1994) include the following:

1. *Organizing groups:* an essential skill of leaders

2. *Negotiating solutions:* mediating, preventing, and resolving conflicts

3. *Personal connection:* empathy and the ability to connect with others and respond appropriately to their feelings and concerns

4. *Social analysis:* the ability to detect and have insights about people's feelings, motives, and concerns

That administrators need such interpersonal skills for their work is well known, and is a part of every textbook on human relations. Every leader has a mental list of what dispositions and skills she considers important for maintaining good relationships with others. These might include the following: collaboration, listening, trust, respect, communication skills, compassion, honesty, conflict resolution skills, sense of humor, openness, conversation, and empathy.

However, such interpersonal abilities need to be balanced by attention to one's own needs and feelings, and how to fulfill those. We learn about ourselves from being with others. In relationships with people at work, we have to practice social skills and maintain a socially acceptable manner. As pointed out in the first chapter of this book, stress often results when there is conflict between one's inner needs, being true to oneself, and the expectations of others that we feel we have to meet. Have you ever known an administrator who is so concerned about maintaining social approval that you wonder who he really is as a person?

To keep an appropriate balance between expressing how we truly feel and what a social situation demands is not easy. The conflicts and dysfunctions that can occur in relationships are as endless as the range of variances in human nature. Next time you're in a bookstore, visit the section on relationships. You will find hundreds of volumes written about how to have a better relationship with your spouse, partner, children, or lover, as well as numerous books on dating, sex, and couples.

Since the purpose of this chapter is to talk about how relationships with others help us with our Personal Growth, let's talk a bit about something psychologists call boundaries.

SELF AND OTHERS

Boundaries are a basic dynamic in any relationship. Dr. Charles Whitfield (1993) says that having an awareness of boundaries and limits is crucial to having healthy relationships. Knowing one's inner life (beliefs, thoughts, feelings, decisions, choices, experiences, needs), discovering who I am, is key to developing good relationships with others. Whitfield states, "The more I get to know my True Self [which he also calls the Child Within] and its inner life clearly, the more I will likely know what is actually mine in any relationship" (p. 82).

Spending time with others who are safe helps us experience our own inner dynamics. Safe others would include family members and friends. We can let down our hair (our boundaries) with them, be comfortable and spontaneous with them, and learn about ourselves when we're with them. Talking it out is one of the ways recommended by the National Association for Mental Health as a way to deal with tensions (Carr, 1974, p. 25). Psychologists tell us that we need to pay attention to what makes us angry when we are with others, as that often reveals a shadow, namely something in our unconscious that is unresolved, that we are hiding from ourselves.

Remember when we talked about stress and crises in chapter 1? Can you remember a time when life gave you one of those unfair and incomprehensible deals that threw you into an abyss of confusion or depression?

Did you have a special someone who helped you through it? You are lucky if you had a trusted friend.

Being alone at such a time is bad for your health. Goleman (1995, p. 179) describes a 7-year study, published in 1993, of all (752) men in Goeteborg, Sweden who were born in 1933. In the 7 years, 41 had died. Men who had originally reported being under intense emotional stress had a death rate three times greater than those who said their lives were calm and placid. "Yet among men who said they had a dependable web of intimacy—a wife, close friends, and the like—there was no relationship whatever between high stress levels and death rate." Having people to turn to protected them. If you have such a friend or a family member, you are blessed!

Here is a noteworthy list of life areas that may be shared in relationships (Whitfield, 1993, p. 131):

1. *Social:* sharing a group experience

2. *Intellectual:* sharing ideas or thoughts

3. *Emotional:* sharing feelings

4. *Physical:* working together

5. *Recreational:* sharing a recreational activity

6. *Aesthetic:* sharing what is beautiful or artistic

7. *Affectional:* sharing affection through touch or tenderness or special caring

8. *Sexual:* requires a prior relationship; deep closeness is possible

9. *Spiritual:* sharing a spiritual experience

YOUR INNER OTHERS

Sometimes even the best friends don't understand. Sometimes you have to go through it alone. That's when you meet your inner others.

Mike was dean at his college. In another month he would no longer be there. His head was swimming with all that had happened. It involved politics, the bureaucracy, and his best friend stabbing him in the back. It was a nightmare! His wife had been distancing herself from him and had gone to live with her parents. Mike had been a successful public school administrator prior to coming to the university and, as with many administrators, he had been an extrovert. What happened to him now sent him to an inner world of turmoil where he met his inner enemies—and, in time, would learn to meet his inner friends.

The whole notion that there were inner others was quite foreign to Mike. His brother, an introvert, had undergone years of analysis and was very comfortable talking about that world. Mike's inner world was like a fog to him. He had always related better (and very well, he thought) to people in the outside world. The only thing he felt now was that he was lost and that there was an inner enemy, an inner monster, who was attacking him with feelings of guilt, shame, and worthlessness. In time he learned to see other characters in the fog and the thicket of his inner forest, thanks to seeing a psychologist and joining a therapy group. He learned to look inside himself, become more inner-oriented. Once he dreamed about an island to which he fled to escape from his inner monsters. He met some people there who became his friends, his guides, and to whom he could turn when others around him couldn't help. As time passed, his inner monsters visited him less frequently in his dreams. It took him several years, but Mike became a new person, had a new career, became more balanced in his work, and paid more attention to his inner world.

Maybe Mike's story sounds strange to you, but psychologists and spiritual leaders have long made us aware of that important inner world: The characters there include the archetypes from our collective unconscious (C. G. Jung), inner demons and angels, our own shadow parts, the presence of a higher power within us (depending on your belief system), and our child within, about which some psychologists have written in recent years. Silence and meditation, spending times alone or with others, paying attention to our dream symbols—all of this helps us get to know what's inside us.

HOW RELATIONSHIPS CONTRIBUTE TO OUR PERSONAL GROWTH

Try some of the following suggestions. I want to acknowledge the inspiration I have received for such activities from the book *Everyday Serenity* (Kundtz, 2000) and would recommend your reading this work for additional ideas.

Just sit still with a friend some time. Nothing needs to happen in the silence between you. Listen to your heart, absorb the silence, and be aware of the unspoken feelings between you.

Take time for a real conversation. Take time to give a thoughtful, unhurried reply. Turn off the TV and stay at the dinner table a little longer.

Become aware of what your kids are saying that might reflect your excuses for overwork, for not spending enough time with them. Pay attention to how they perceive you living your life.

Make eye contact with someone for more than a second. Is there an inner connection? Take a risk to connect with someone.

How much are you doing for other people when you don't really want to and when you resent it? Are you overcommitting to others' needs? Do you feel responsible for everyone's suffering? You may need to set some healthy boundaries in your relationships.

Can you cry with someone? Can you let someone cry and just sit with her? When someone expresses sadness or shares a problem, resist sharing your own similar situation; just be silently receptive to your friend. You can always tell her later.

Antisthenes, a fourth-century Greek philosopher said, "Pay attention to your enemies, for they are the first to discover your mistakes." People who oppose you, who don't see things as you do, may help you see hidden parts of yourself, and let you know where you need to grow.

Tell someone, "I love you." I have noticed that this is increasingly becoming part of a standard greeting in many families. I believe that this kind of openness, unknown in my youth and native culture, is a good trend. Tell those whom you have appreciated in your life how important they are to you. Do it now!

Do you allow verbal abuse of yourself, or of others in your presence? Have the courage to say, "Stop it!" Forgiveness is a good spiritual goal, but so is stopping injustice.

Pay attention to the old wisdom and spiritual law that what is within you will be expressed to the world. Make time for silence and notice what is within you. Learn to be quiet enough to hear the sound of the genuine within yourself so that you can hear it in others (Marian Wright Edelman, quoted in Kundtz, 2000, p. 342).

I will conclude with a quote from one of those wonderful books on friendship (Lovric, 1993) that one of my friends gave me a long time ago (you might look for one for a friend in your bookstore).

> Oh, the comfort, the inexpressible comfort
> of feeling safe with a person;
> having neither to weigh thoughts nor
> measure words,
> but pour them out, just as they are,
> chaff and grain together,
> Knowing that a faithful hand will take and
> sift them,

keep what is worth keeping,
And then with the breath of kindness, blow
the rest away.

—Dinah Maria Mulock Craik
(1826–1887), English Writer

REFLECTIONS AND EXERCISES

1. When you're with someone you love, become aware of your own feelings. What makes you angry? Upset? Disappointed? Then ask yourself, "Why is this bothering me? Why am I letting this person bug me?" Go deep inside yourself and see what part of you is hurting. Write an inner dialogue with that part of you.

2. Take the list of life areas shared in relationships in this chapter and reflect on how you share these with a special friend or family member. If there are some of them that you are not sharing, ask yourself "why not" and reflect on that.

3. Reflect on the old proverb: "Make new friends, but keep the old. They are silver, the others gold." Make a list of your silver and golden friends. What are you doing to keep your valued friendships alive? Which do you feel you need to drop?

4. Look again at the list in the beginning of this chapter of activities that you could do with others. Make a plan to include some of these each day or week in your life.

5. List the important people in your life. What is the special meaning each has for your own Personal Growth? How much time are you spending with each? What are you doing to nourish each of your significant relationships?

6. Ask a trusted friend to give you feedback on your body language and what it communicates to others.

7. Dialogue with yourself: In my relationships, do I practice what I preach? Who are my role models, my heroes (Jesus, Buddha, my grandmother, parent, child, business associate, a great statesman, a philosopher or spiritual leader), and does my daily life reflect their values?

11

Fulfilling Your Purpose as a Leader and Finding Meaning as a Person

Connection is not something you do. It's a profound awareness of how you actually live your life.

—Paul Pearsall

Stephen Covey in his book *The 8th Habit* (2004), extends a leadership challenge (his 8th habit) which allows leaders to move from effectiveness to greatness: "The crucial challenge of our world today is to find your voice and inspire others to find their voice . . . Leadership is communicating to people their worth and potential so clearly that they come to see it themselves" (p. 98). Covey says to do this, we need spiritual intelligence, which he defines as our drive for meaning and connection with the infinite.

We have come full circle from the beginning of this book. To be the kind of leader who can move to greatness, you must know how to take care of yourself and connect with others through your leadership responsibilities. This book has outlined a number of ways you can begin to do this.

"So," you ask, "how do I make this connection between what I do in my personal life and my work life? How is what I'm doing for my Personal Growth going to affect my work? How can I affect the lives of those with whom I work? How can I incorporate these practices into my work?"

The answer is actually rather simple. I will use a familiar metaphor from nature, a living plant. If you water and nourish the soil of the plant, so that the roots are deep and strong, the plant will grow. It will sprout leaves, bloom, and bear its fruit. That is the way of nature, and it is also a spiritual law. If you nurture your inner roots through some of the practices discussed in this book, there will be an outer consequence. There will be a harvest that will be evident in all areas of your life. Sound too simple?

The theory and principles behind this law are reliable, predictable, and straightforward; however, in practice, this process is anything but linear and smooth. In fact, it is messy and uncertain, with setbacks, spurts forward, and a lot of wondering how you're doing with it. Just as in the life of a plant there will be dead leaves, broken branches, rotting fruit, and some buds that never open; thus it is with our own inner journey to wholeness, to balance. The Personal Growth practices will cultivate and nourish the soil, and the wind and weather of life's experiences will whip the leaves and shape the plant.

Let's talk a bit more about this connection between using these practices and the result in the leader's outer life.

CONNECTING PERSONAL GROWTH PRACTICES WITH WORK

Many authors have talked about the impact of the leader's Personal Development on her work. Everyone agrees on how important this connection is. Yet, too many of us see our personal and professional lives as separate. We use our intellect (our head) at work, but we feel fragmented and divided from our emotions, our spirit, our soul (our heart). We see our home life and our work life as distinct and detached. Even if you have begun to incorporate some of the practices described in this book, you may see them more as a part of your personal life. Even though what you do for yourself, and who you are as a person, will impact who you are at work, it will be a challenge to connect the two. Goleman (1995) says that the intellect cannot work its best without emotional intelligence and urges us to harmonize head and heart (pp. 28–29). "Show me how I can do that," you say.

Here are some books about leaders and organizations in general that may be useful for you to read. One is the new *8th Habit* book by Steven

Covey (2004) already mentioned above. Another book that reports on research of spiritual practices in the corporate world is Mitroff and Denton's (1999) A *Spiritual Audit of Corporate America*. Julia Cameron (*The Artist's Way*, 1992) and two coauthors (Bryan, Cameron, & Allen, 1998) wrote a book to address this topic: *The Artist's Way at Work: Riding the Dragon*. They use the ancient symbol of the dragon to depict transformation toward enlightenment. This book takes you on a 12-week emotional, mental, and spiritual journey to apply the principles of personal creativity to the work environment. Michael Thompson's *The Congruent Life* (2000) is an important work that explores the search for meaning in our lives and as leaders of our organizations. A newly revised book by Koestenbaum (2002), *Leadership: The Inner Side of Greatness—A Philosophy for Leaders,* uses stories about leaders' professional experiences to reflect on practice and to articulate values and beliefs in leaders' decision-making. And then there is the one that has become almost a classic, *Leading With Soul* (Bolman & Deal, 1995).

But what about this connection as it applies specifically to leaders in educational work environments?

PERSONAL GROWTH PRACTICES IN THE EDUCATIONAL ENVIRONMENT

In my surveys and interviews of school leaders, I asked the question about how these Personal Growth principles and practices might be applied in schools. In what follows, I have incorporated the suggestions from school principals, superintendents, and other administrators for including Personal Growth practices in administrative preparation programs, in professional development programs, and for building them into the culture and daily life of the organization.

INCORPORATE PERSONAL GROWTH PRACTICES INTO PREPARATION PROGRAMS FOR SCHOOL ADMINISTRATORS

The dispositions of leaders (defined in chapter 2 as including a person's traits, character, and personal qualities) are commonly referred to in national and state standards for school administrators. They must be included in coursework and in practical fieldwork experiences of people preparing to be administrators. Some universities have recently been incorporating courses on ethics (related to character) for educational leaders in their preparation programs. The current emphasis on assessment in preparation programs has generated discussion among university faculty and researchers surrounding the measurement of traits and personal qualities needed by administrators. Such dialogue is a healthy beginning. It needs to be continued and should involve both practitioners and university faculty.

As a good example of the growing awareness of the importance of this topic, the most current California Standards of Quality and Effectiveness for Preliminary Administrative Services Credential Programs include the following elements (Category III, Standard 14):

> Each candidate knows how to sustain personal motivation, commitment, energy, and health by balancing professional and personal responsibilities (g)
>
> Each candidate engages in professional and *personal development* (h) [italics mine]

This book might provide a good supplement and an important balance to the traditional university textbooks, which cover mainly knowledge and skills of administrators.

INCLUDE PERSONAL GROWTH PRACTICES IN PROFESSIONAL DEVELOPMENT (INSERVICE) PROGRAMS

The following topics were suggested as staff development sessions related to Personal Growth that might be included: stress management; time management; the personal competencies (dispositions) needed for success by school leaders; ethical dimensions of leadership; strategies such as book clubs or brown bag lunches where books or experiences about such topics are read and discussed in small groups; crisis management (personal and professional); listening skills; self-management; enhanced personal creativity and problem-solving capacity; interpersonal support; humor; self-renewal; and creating a culture of interpersonal support.

To this list I would add that administrators need workshops that enhance other types of intelligences, such as spiritual intelligence (Covey, 1989, 2004) and emotional intelligence (Goleman, 1995). Hands-on sessions that help administrators use their "right brain" would be beneficial not only for their Personal Growth, but also for improving creative problem-solving and decision-making capacities. And finally, what would be wrong with a workshop on how to meditate, as some corporations are doing for their executives?

INTEGRATE PERSONAL GROWTH PRACTICES INTO THE CULTURE OF THE ORGANIZATION

The suggestion most frequently mentioned was that the leader must lead by example. The leader must be a role model for building such practices into his own daily life. The people in the school organization and school community must perceive the leader as someone who

- is a self-reflective person who models taking care of himself
- takes time for herself and for others
- sets priorities for use of time that are based on their core values
- takes care of his physical body, his total health
- is seen reading inspirational and spiritual books, and encourages others in this
- uses words and behaves in a manner that exemplifies her life values
- visibly practices the values of her organization, as stated in the vision and mission statements
- is perceived as taking time to be centered and present with people and situations
- acknowledges her own inner life (feelings, thoughts, ideas, choices, beliefs)
- recognizes and respects the inner life of others
- values creative thinking, intuition, and diversity
- engages in creative work himself and supports it in others
- is perceived as practicing a balance between times of silence and being with others
- pursues her dreams and encourages others to do the same
- mentors and gives feedback to others in their Personal Growth efforts
- opens his mind and heart before making a judgment or decision
- makes Personal Growth practices a part of the little things of every-day life at work

Here are some specific and personal comments made by school administrators that may stimulate and expand your own ideas:

- I try to create a comfortable and beautiful environment around me and others. I always try to have some fresh flowers around, arrange the furniture to be open and inviting, and watch that bulletin boards don't become junky looking. I always have some refreshments around for people. I want my school grounds to be litter free and a pleasant environment for the people who work here.

- I have a couple of pieces of paper always on my desk where I can see them: "In God I trust. I am not afraid. What can people do to me?"

- I always carry the prayer of Theresa of Avila with me:

> Let nothing disturb me,
> Let nothing make me afraid.
> All things are passing,
> God alone never changes.
> Patience endures.
> He who has God
> Will want for nothing,
> God alone suffices.

- I have a sign behind my name plate at school board meetings. It's the Swahili word for journey: WGASA. It says to me Who Gives A S—T Anyway? (From a superintendent with a good sense of humor.)

- I go out and shoot hoops with the kids when I need a break. I relax when I sit in a classroom observing teachers and kids. I love working with the children.

- I close my door and spend a few seconds in silence before I have a stressful meeting or a difficult conference.

- I look at balance in two ways: my life outside of work and what I do in my job. I find the things within my job that I enjoy and do those as much as I can. I enjoy being with the kids, planning with teachers, sometimes teaching in the classroom.

- I find ways to make the job easier for teachers. For example, when the district sends us some compliance guidelines that can "kill you," I create graphs or charts to make it more comprehensible and fun to complete.

The interviews and survey comments highlighted the difficulty in using Personal Growth practices on the job. One principal told me that the only time during the day he has alone is while he is on his 10- to 15-minute lunch break at his desk. The stress created by not having someone to share and talk things out with at work was mentioned by several, especially when there is only one administrator in the school. The time constraints seemed to be the biggest issue. One principal said, "Every time the district has some kind of blue ribbon committee to reduce our workload, it seems to increase."

You might also enjoy looking at a wonderful list of simple, everyday ideas that readers submitted to the journal *Spirituality & Health* (Scott, 2002), entitled "Fifty Ways to Nourish Your Soul."

PERSONAL GROWTH IS A JOURNEY, NOT A DESTINATION

This concept has been implied throughout the book, but now needs to be explicitly stated. If you don't internalize this statement, you may lose patience with yourself and give up. Changing habits is a very difficult process. But then we wouldn't be in education if we didn't believe that it is possible to change attitudes and behavior—even in adults.

It should be emphasized that you can't change your attitude, behavior, or habits just by your own willpower, through your own ego. I believe that it is essential to enlist the aid of a power higher than your ego (call it God, your higher Self, or what you will). I'm not saying that it's impossible to make changes without such a belief in something or someone outside of yourself, but I do know that the danger of self-deception in this process is great. Continuous vigilance is required. Support from somewhere inside you, as well as outside of you, is essential. We cannot underestimate the value of talking with a trained professional, a psychologist, a spiritual leader, or someone in a support group. Such persons can assist us, give us feedback, encourage us, and, when needed, keep us from being inflated about our "progress."

To express what is within you to the world, you need to take the first steps, which Kundtz (2000) lists as "time, quietude, and peace to notice and appreciate what is within" (p. 349). In our first chapter we talked about the stressful nature of the job. Have you become more aware of how you react to stressful events? Have you spent some time reflecting or meditating on how you might react in a more wholesome way? Are you learning to open up to a new way coming from your inner wisdom? Then practice it, one insight at a time.

A journey takes place one step at a time. Select one area of your life that you want to change and work on that. Use the practices in this book.

For example, let's go back to Principal Steve in the first chapter. There are a number of changes Steve will want to make, but he might select "finding time for jogging again" as his first one. Maybe he will do walking instead, but he will make a plan to build in time for some exercise two or three times a week. He can experiment with different times during the week, and it doesn't have to be a rigid schedule. He will want to consider his other priorities, such as family events or evening meetings. Another thing Steve might do is to be more creative in how he meets his deadlines. He can become more aware of how he organizes his time to begin earlier on projects, such as the safety report he had to complete. Steve will get to know himself better, so that he can recognize signs of stress more quickly. He will know what practices work best for him to stay centered, and to take care of his inner self as he faces the daily rush of stressful job situations. For another look at Steve, turn to the Resource notes of this chapter ("A Day in the Life of a Balanced Leader").

WHAT PRACTICES ARE MOST IMPORTANT AND HOW CAN I BEGIN?

You might ask which of the practices are absolutely essential and might have priority on your journey. The ones I would select are described in chapter 8. I believe that spending time in silence and meditation, even for short periods, formally or informally, is key to many of the other practices. It is in such moments that you discover what lies within you, who you are, and who you want to be. Developing a habit of centering and focusing, an awareness of what is going on inside and around you in every present moment, is probably the most important practice to develop at first. "In connecting with the wholeness of experience in this moment, you are able to discover what matters most" (Brantley, 2003, p. 176).

You can begin to work on the other practices, depending on your interest and inclination. Whatever of these practices you use, just remember to make them work for your Personal Growth. This means being mindful and intentional in whatever you're doing. Here are some suggestions:

- You can immediately establish a routine of physical activity of some kind. One principal I interviewed said he tries to get in some exercise by walking around his campus as briskly as possible. He knows he has to take his pager or cell phone, but hopes he won't get too many interruptions during his walking time.
- You can buy a journal and keep track of your ideas, dreams, and reflections.
- You can become more considerate of your body and notice when a headache is beginning. Then be good to yourself and take a break: Go and look out of the window for a few minutes or water the plants

in your office. Be good to your body and start watching what you put into it.

- Reflect as you do an art project or a creative hobby. Take time to put it together with love and passion.
- While listening to music, let it create an inner harmony. Maybe you'll experience a storm of emotions as you listen to the tender beauty of Beethoven's ninth symphony, which he wrote when he was already completely deaf. Let yourself feel the sadness as you hear Brahms's Requiem, reminding you of the parent or child you lost. Touch the sky with a joy beyond this world that a favorite choral piece might inspire.
- Go to a play or sporting event and focus on not thinking about anything else, especially work stress.
- You can go and buy one of the books recommended here, and begin by reading in it a bit every chance you get. In time, when you find what works best for you, you will want to develop a regular reading habit for your spiritual and inspirational books.
- You can become aware of how much time you are, or are not, spending with friends and family and make a plan to connect with those important people in your life.
- You can analyze how you spend your time at work, prioritize your activities, and set a time when you will be finished with a task. As one principal said in my interview: "I will determine when I'm done. I'll set a goal—let's say 20 minutes—for doing this paperwork, and then go home. Whatever is not done will wait."

A DAY IN THE LIFE OF A BALANCED LEADER

There was a question in the first chapter about what a leader who takes care of himself would look like. I have included in the Resource notes for this chapter such a description. If you would like to read about an "enlightened," more balanced Principal Steve—but one who still has his stresses and struggles—turn to his story. It is important to remember about this being a process, not an idealized state of being that someone reaches at some point in his life. It is also understood that each administrator will adapt the practices to suit his or her unique needs and lifestyle.

I hope you will resolve to do something different in your life. Make yourself a priority! Decide to create a balance in your life, to engage in your Personal Growth and be better as a leader for others. The rewards will be great!

REFLECTIONS AND EXERCISES

1. How will times of silence, times alone, times in meditation (formal and informal) help you? Build such times into your daily schedule. Write your insights and reflections.

2. Review the Personal Growth practices described in this book and listed below. Make several copies of this Personal Growth Plan chart. Write a specific activity you plan to do for one or more of them during a particular week or month.

3. After you have tried each of the practices, write some reflections about what happened. Then make a list of which ones you want to continue. Enlist the support of a friend and/or family member. Make a plan to build these into your personal and professional life. Set a weekly schedule for these and continue to reflect on them by writing notes on the chart or in your journal.

4. Most importantly, determine to be patient with yourself! Don't give up if you didn't meet your goals. Just keep working at them. As long as you are convinced of the importance of these practices for yourself, you will make them a part in your life. In time you will find what works best for your Personal Growth.

5. Write this affirmation on a card and keep it where you can see it:

   "I am patient with myself on my journey to become a better leader and a more balanced person."

Date: _____

Personal Growth Plan

Times in silence

Solitude—times alone

Meditation

Something related to art

Something related to music

Writing (journal or other personal writing)

Fulfilling a dream

Keeping track and analyzing what I dream

Physical exercise

Reflective reading

Spending time with family

Spending time with friends

Managing my time at work for my own Personal Growth

Resource Notes for Chapter 2

WORDS USED IN THE WORKPLACE

Table R.1   Keeping Track

Terms used in the workplace	How often used in your organization—mark a tally when you hear or use it	How often used in your organization—rank from 1to11
Values		
Ethics		
Heart		
Love		
Morals		
Spirit		
Meaning of life		
Soul		
Spirituality		

Resource Notes for Chapter 3

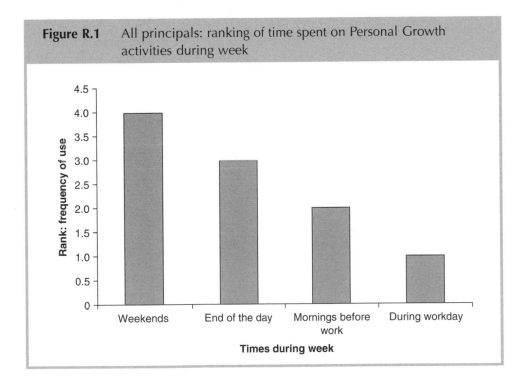

Figure R.1 All principals: ranking of time spent on Personal Growth activities during week

Figure R.2   Administrators (all levels): time spent on Personal Growth activities

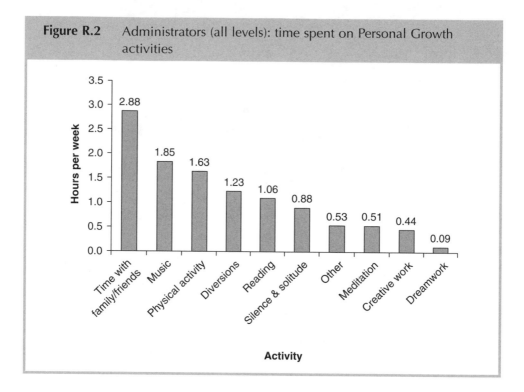

Table R.2   Time Analysis Worksheet*

TASK	7:00	8:00	9:00	10:00	11:00	12:00	1:00	2:00	3:00	4:00	5:00	6:00	7:00	
Planning														
Scheduling														
Interviewing														
Meeting														
Conference w. superior														
Employee conference														
Correspondence														
Record keeping														
Filing														
Telephone														
Facilities problem														
Studying data														
Lunch/breakfast														
Break period														

(Continued)

Table R.2 (Continued)

TASK	7:00	8:00	9:00	10:00	11:00	12:00	1:00	2:00	3:00	4:00	5:00	6:00	7:00	
Visiting														
Idle time														
Waiting time														
Instructional supervision														
Solving technical problem														
Personal Growth														

* Try doing one for every half hour or even for every quarter hour.

Resource Notes for Chapter 4

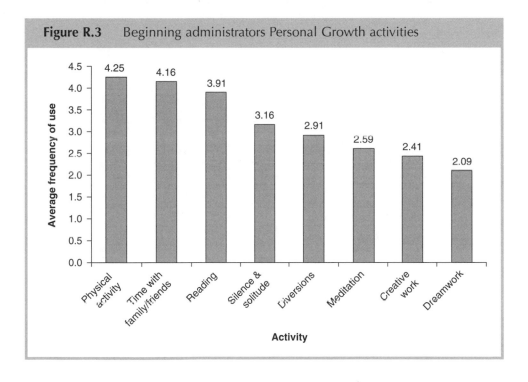

Figure R.3 Beginning administrators Personal Growth activities

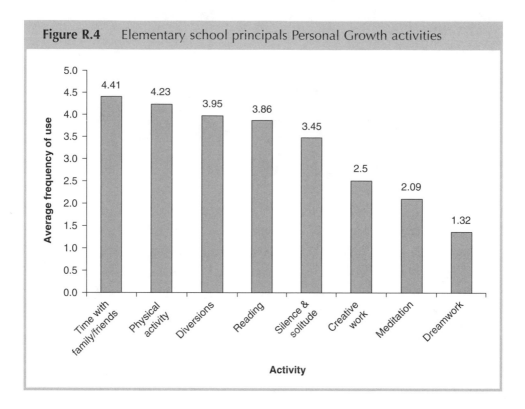

Figure R.4   Elementary school principals Personal Growth activities

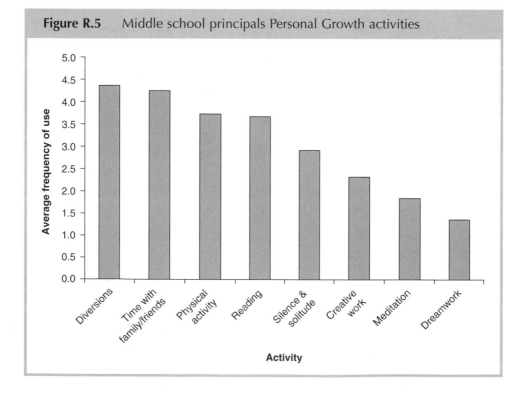

Figure R.5   Middle school principals Personal Growth activities

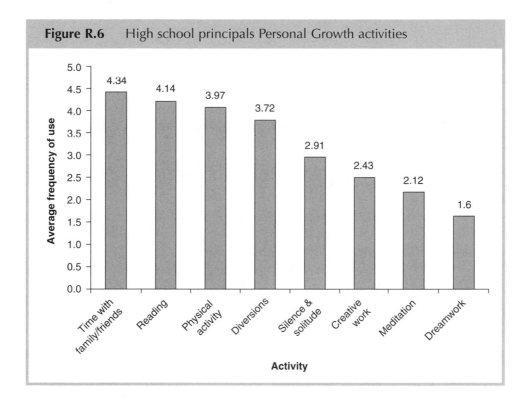

Figure R.6   High school principals Personal Growth activities

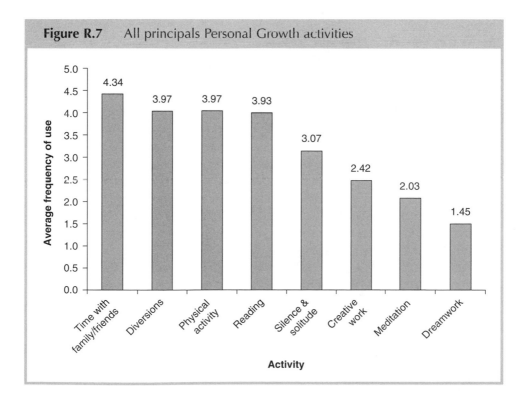

Figure R.7   All principals Personal Growth activities

Resource Notes for Chapter 6

FAVORITE PERSONAL GROWTH BOOKS

Bolman, L. G., & Deal, T. E. (1995). *Leading with soul: An uncommon journey of spirit.* San Francisco: Jossey-Bass.

Brantley, J. (2003). *Calming your anxious mind.* Oakland, CA: New Harbinger.

Covey, S. R. (1989). *The seven habits of highly effective people.* New York: Simon & Schuster.

Johnson, R. R. (1986). *Inner work: Using dreams and active imagination for personal growth.* San Francisco: HarperSanFrancisco.

Kabat-Zinn, J. (1994). *Wherever you go there you are: Mindfulness meditation in everyday life.* New York: Hyperion Books.

Keating, T. (1997). *Open mind, open heart.* New York: The Continuum.

King, S. (1981). *Imagineering for health: Self-healing through the use of the mind.* Wheaton, IL: Quest Books.

Kundtz, D. (2000). *Everyday serenity: Meditations for people who do too much.* New York: MJF Books.

Moore, T. (1992). *Care of the soul: A guide for cultivating depth and sacredness in everyday life.* New York: Harper Perennial.

Thich Nhat Hanh. (1976). *The miracle of mindfulness: A manual on meditation.* Boston: Beacon Press.

Thompson, C. M. (2000). *The congruent life: Following the inward path to fulfilling work and inspired leadership.* San Francisco: Jossey-Bass.

Tolle, E. (1999). *The power of now.* Novato, CA: New World Library.

Resource Notes for Chapter 8

MEDITATION PRACTICE: WHO AM I?

This practice is recommended by Kabat-Zinn (1994) as a useful way to contemplate one's life and linger on such basic questions as "Who am I?" "Where am I going?" "What path am I on?" "What is my yearning, my path?" In this practice, you don't have to come up with answers, nor must you think that there has to be one particular answer. Just persist in asking the question, letting any answers that formulate just come of themselves and go of themselves. "As with everything else in the meditation practice, we just watch, listen, note, let be, let go, and keep generating the question, 'What is my Way? Who am I?'" (p. 132).

This meditation could work either in a space and time set aside for it, or as a question that may stay with you throughout your day. It will help you to get to know yourself better and to be more conscious of the reasons for your choices. Why am I experiencing a particular emotion in a particular situation? What is my motivation for action? Why does a certain person's behavior annoy and "stress" me? What are my values, my beliefs on which I will base my decision? Only by first becoming aware of and reflecting on such questions can you change aspects of your behavior that you may want to change.

Resource Notes
for Chapter 11

A DAY IN THE LIFE OF A BALANCED LEADER

What might Principal Steve's day look like after
he has worked on his Personal Growth for a while (and has read this book)?

Steve gets up at 5:30, about 15 minutes earlier than he used to. Because his family is still asleep, he quietly heads for his study. He stretches his limbs and gets the blood flowing to help him focus on being present to this new day. He is conscious of his breathing as he does each exercise. He knows tomorrow is his regular hour at the fitness center, but he wants to remind his body daily in some way to stay flexible and strong. When he first began creating this special time for himself, he tried it in the evenings before bedtime. However, as a general rule, mornings seem to work better for him.

After a few minutes of physical exercise, he heads for a chair that looks out into his backyard. That is his special place, reserved for times when he needs to meditate or just to reflect on something. From here he can see the hills surrounding the city. The soft glow of the rising sun is framing the branches of the pine tree outside his window. Sometimes he lights a candle. Sitting there always means the same thing and has an immediate effect on him: Be quiet and alone for a while.

When he has time, mostly just on weekends, he sits for a longer time and practices one of his meditations. He's found that the longer time (he aims for 20 minutes) helps him to become centered more quickly at times like today, when he only has 5 minutes to sit. Sometimes in the evenings, when he needs to relax, he sits for a while and turns on his favorite music. This helps him to let the worries of the day recede into the melody and float away like a boat down a river.

He knows the importance of those few minutes. They help him get grounded in what is important in his life. As he sits, thoughts arise of what is ahead of him that day. He is practicing to allow them just to pass by. He doesn't focus on them, or get emotionally involved with them. He knows that when the events of the day come, he will know what to do. Sometimes he doesn't succeed very well because the issue grips him too strongly. It helps him to close his eyes. He breathes deeply and begins to focus on his center. He sits until he feels grounded and calm. If there is any concern remaining in his mind, he allows it to move into his heart until he knows that all will be well. He is ready for the day. One last glance at the golden morning sky outside and he proceeds to do his morning chores.

After a healthy breakfast and the usual family rituals, he decides that he won't need his car today, but will ride the metro to school. He knows that he won't be able to take the usual noon walk around the track at his school today because the superintendent has scheduled a meeting for right after lunch. So the brisk walk to the station, and then to his school, might be the only walking exercise he will get today.

When he arrives at school, the fun begins! Things never stop moving, problems keep coming, and people keep needing him all day long. Steve is motivated by the pace, and time passes quickly. He sighs when a teacher tells him a particularly poignant story. So much suffering, so many unfinished dreams! Sometimes he feels overwhelmed and helpless in the face of all he is expected to do, and be, for so many people: teachers, staff, parents, politicians, colleagues, and, most importantly, his students. He tries to be aware that anyone he meets that day may need an understanding smile.

As he confronts each situation, his mind springs into action to decide what is the best way to approach a particular individual, and the best way to solve a problem. He knows that he has been blessed with a good intellect, but he has also been practicing to stop for a little longer before making a decision to examine what is in his heart. And he is learning to live with unresolved issues that used to stress him out.

As he walks around his school and visits classrooms, he allows his senses to be in touch with the surroundings. He is aware of the sights and smells around him, and of each individual with whom he comes in contact. This helps him remain focused on the highest priorities of each moment. If he could just be better at not allowing the burden of anxious thoughts to weigh down his mind! His thoughts always seem to want to jump ahead, or to look back on what he might have done or should do. It helps him to look up at the clouds sometimes as he walks around. The spacious sky gives him a wider perspective on whatever is going on at the moment.

At lunchtime he sits with the teachers in the lounge for a few minutes to eat a bite. He visits the cafeteria and roams the playgrounds, stopping to answer questions or making notes of things that need to be taken care of. Since he is the only administrator at his school, he always takes his two-way radio. When he is on his usual noon walk on the field (sometimes accompanied by a teacher or his nurse), his staff knows to contact him only for extremely urgent matters.

After the students have gone back into their classrooms, he closes his office door for a few minutes to collect his papers, but mostly his mind, for the meeting ahead. He still has a problem with the numerous meetings called by other people. So often they seem to be a waste of time and he knows he will be tempted to speak up and ask too many questions about a particularly senseless mandate or unrealistic report deadline. For his own meetings, he has learned to reduce the number by using e-mail or personal contact, except when full discussion of an issue needs to take place with all views heard.

A neighboring principal picks him up and the few minutes they have to chat on the way do him good. He misses not having an assistant with whom he can share thoughts and ideas. They talk about the impact on their schools of what they will surely hear in the meeting today, namely the consequences of not making their adequate yearly progress on test scores. They worry about the many limited English speakers and their special education students who have to be tested right along with all the others. To them, these students and their teachers are not just statistics in some accountability manual, but real people whose lives are impacted by policies and laws.

At 3:00, he returns to his school, just in time for student dismissal. This is always a hectic time and can become stressful, but it's also a rewarding time. He likes the smiles of farewell, the shouts of recognition, especially from the younger children. He greets the parents picking up their children and always gets a bit crazy with the traffic congestion in front of the school. He tries not to think about the many times he's sent home notices to parents about where the preferred pick-up place is to be. He checks to make sure the designated supervisors are at their assigned duties. One of the aides, Mrs. Payson, is late again. He's got to figure out how he can help her improve, or he will have to begin the process of documenting for dismissal. Since she is the wife of a school board member in the neighboring district, it won't be easy.

By 4:30, most of the teachers have left for the day. He hopes to get some paperwork done, but knows that there will always be a few who are waiting to talk to him. He checks his in-basket and e-mail and replies to the most important items. He prints out other e-mails that he can put into a folder as a reminder to take care of later on. At 5:30 he starts to clear his desk. It's not easy to leave because there's still so much to do. But he knows that there will always be more to do than time allows. On the days when he goes to the gym (he tries for at least one evening a week and one hour on the weekends), he leaves an hour earlier. His priority tonight is to get home for dinner with his family.

He makes stacks of the things on his desk: The "A" pile that has to be done first thing tomorrow, folders by project or topic to be done later, a drawer for things to do when time, and the trash can for the rest. He is a bit compulsive about recording his to-do list items in his calendar, or in his palm pilot, before he leaves at the end of each day. He loves crossing items off when completed. He writes a brief reminder in the space for the date when he must begin working on the report from today's meeting so that he will get it done by the deadline. He knows that once something is written down, it will be easier to let it go from his mind.

When he leaves a little after 6:00, he wants his mind to be uncluttered with the routine to-do things and to allow some space for creative problem solving on major issues. The matter with Mrs. Payson is weighing heavily on him. He will need to use all of his mental and inner resources to know what to do. But right now he needs to focus on clearing his mind.

As he is walking to the metro stop, a nice surprise greets him: His wife is picking him up. They chat for a few minutes, exchanging events of their days. Although he is tired ("exhausted" might be a better word), his mind is lucid and his heart is open for her and for the stories of the children at home.

They have supper together and he fulfills his duties by helping with clearing away the food and dishes. He encourages his children to complete their homework before bedtime. He heads for his study and for his reflection chair. He mentally reviews the past day. He has met the challenges of that day, and knows there will be more tomorrow. By that time of the evening, his thoughts of work are generally put to rest. He resists the urge to write down ideas or solutions to work problems (especially about what to do with Mrs. Payson) because this habit has not been good for him. He used to keep a pad by his bedside and would wake up all night making notes on thoughts that occurred to him. Whenever he read his ideas in the morning, they weren't all that brilliant anyway. It was more important for him to go back to sleep (the "breathing in, breathing out" technique seems to work well for him). He is better about that now and trusts himself that such insights will come back to him, if they are good ones.

There is still an hour left before bedtime. What a wonderful gift this hour is! He can fill it with whatever he chooses: work on his hobby, have a talk with his wife, call a friend, take an evening walk, read a magazine, go for a swim at the gym, or even (when he's really worn out) watch TV for a while. Such free time is a real luxury for him and he deeply appreciates it. When he has evening meetings or school events that he must attend, he has to rely on his weekends to find, or create, such precious hours—or even just minutes— for himself.

Before he goes to sleep, he reads a few pages from his favorite (nonprofessional) book and reflects a bit on his life. Yes, he likes being an administrator. He is learning to pace himself, to balance his work and his personal life. His responses to stresses are getting much more wholesome. He feels grateful for the opportunity to make a difference in the lives of the people he touches, although he still worries whether he can ever do enough.

Steve wakes up that night with a dream. He found himself in a large building that seemed to have no exits. He felt frustration and fear. As he reflected on his dream, he knew what it meant. He had to continue to be vigilant to make sure that his work didn't close in on him, that it didn't imprison him.

His dream made him renew his commitment to always keep a way open to those aspects of his life that connected him with personal freedom, with the essence of his being, with the inner spaces that still needed so much exploring. He knew he needed to always make time for that which was really important in his life, and to stay on his path toward wholeness and balance as a person and administrator.

References

Adams, J. P. (1999, September/October). Good principals, good schools: Survey of CSUN California Preliminary Administrative Services Credential Holders. *Thrust for Educational Leadership, 29*(1), 8–11.

Adler, M. J., & Van Doren, C. (1972). *How to read a book: The classic guide to intelligent reading.* New York: Simon & Schuster.

Anderton, B. (2003). *Meditation exercises and inspirations for well-being.* New York: Barnes & Noble.

Arieti, S. (1976). *Creativity: The magic synthesis.* New York: Basic Books.

Arnold, J. C. (2002). *Escape routes for people who feel trapped in life's hells.* Farmington, PA: The Plough Publishing House.

Au, W., & Cannon, N. (1995). *Urgings of the heart: A spirituality of integration.* New York: Paulist Press.

Benson, H. (with Klipper, M. Z.). (1975). *The relaxation response.* New York: William Morrow.

Benson, H. (with Klipper, M. Z.). (2000). *The relaxation response* (Rev. ed.). New York: HarperTorch.

Block, P. (1993). *Stewardship: Choosing service over self-interest.* San Francisco: Berrett-Koehler.

Bloom, G. (2004, June). Emotionally intelligent principals. *The School Administrator, 61*(6), 14–17.

Bloom, H. (2000). *How to read and why.* New York: Scribner.

Bolman, L. G., & Deal, T. E. (1995). *Leading with soul: An uncommon journey of spirit.* San Francisco: Jossey-Bass.

Brantley, J. (2003). *Calming your anxious mind.* Oakland, CA: New Harbinger.

Bridges, W. (1991). *Managing transitions: Making the most of change.* Reading, MA: Perseus Books.

Briskin, A. (1996). *The stirring of soul in the workplace.* San Francisco: Jossey–Bass.

Brown, J. L., & Moffett, C. A. (1999). *The hero's journey: How educators can transform schools and improve learning.* Alexandria, VA: Association for Supervision and Curriculum Development.

Bryan, M., Cameron, J., & Allen, C. (1998). *The artist's way at work: Riding the dragon.* New York: Quill William Morrow.

Cameron, J. (1992). *The artist's way: A spiritual path to higher creativity.* New York: G. P. Putnam's Sons.

Campbell, D. (1997). *The Mozart effect: Tapping the power of music to heal the body, strengthen the mind, and unlock the creative spirit.* New York: Avon.

Carr, R. (1974). *The yoga way to release tension: Techniques for relaxation and mind control.* New York: Coward, McCann & Geoghegan.

Chevalier, J., & Gheerbrant, A. (1996). *Dictionary of symbols.* London: Penguin.

Chopra, D. (1994). *The seven spiritual laws of success: A practical guide to the fulfillment of your dreams.* San Rafael, CA: Amber-Allen.

Cohn, C. (2001, July 9). Administrator shortage task force outlines strategies. *Association of California School Administrators EdCal, 31*(2), 1, 3.

Conger, J. A. (1998). *Spirit at work: Discovering the spirituality in leadership.* San Francisco: Jossey-Bass.

Conlin, M. (2004, August 30). Meditation: New research shows that it changes the brain in ways that alleviate stress. *Business Week, 3897,* 136–137.

Conner, J. A. (2004, November/December). To examine the secrets of nature. *Science and Spirit, 15*(6), 68.

Cooper, K. H. (1968). *Aerobics.* New York: Bantam Books.

Covey, S. (2004). *The 8th habit: From effectiveness to greatness.* New York: Free Press.

Covey, S. R. (1989). *The seven habits of highly effective people.* New York: Simon & Schuster.

Craze, R. (2004). *The dictionary of dreams and their meanings: Interpretation and insights into the therapeutic nature of our dreams.* London: Hermes House.

Csikszentmihalyi, M. (1996). *Creativity: Flow and the psychology of discovery and invention.* New York: HarperCollins.

Diaz, A. (1992). *Freeing the creative spirit: Drawing on the power of art to tap the magic and wisdom within.* San Francisco: HarperCollins.

Educational Research Service. (1998). *Is there a shortage of qualified candidates for openings in the principalship: An exploratory study.* Arlington, VA: National Association of Elementary Principals and National Association of Secondary School Principals.

Farhi, D. (2000). *Yoga mind, body, and spirit: A return to wholeness.* New York: Henry Holt.

Frankl, V. E. (1984). *Man's search for meaning.* New York: Pocket Books.

Giammatteo, M. C., & Giammatteo, D. M. (1980). *Executive well-being: Stress and administrators.* Reston, VA: National Association of Secondary School Principals.

Glass, T. E., Bjork, L., & Brunner, C. C. (2000). *The study of the American school superintendency 2000.* Arlington, VA: American Association of School Administrators.

Goldberg, N., & Guest, J. (1986). *Writing down the bones: Freeing the writer within.* Boston: Shambhala.

Goleman, D. (1995). *Emotional intelligence: Why it can matter more than IQ.* New York: Bantam Books.

Goleman, D. (2000). *Working on emotional intelligence.* New York: Bantam Books.

Green, B. (with Gallwey, W. T.). (1986). *The inner game of music.* New York: Anchor Press.

Hall, C. S. (1966). *The meaning of dreams.* New York: McGraw-Hill.

Homan, D., & Pratt, L. C. (2002). *Radical hospitality: Benedict's way of love.* Brewster, MA: Paraclete Press.

Houston, P. D. (2002, September). Why spirituality, and why now? *The School Administrator, 59*(8), 6–8.

Jaeger, W. (1995). *Search for the meaning of life: Essays and reflections on the mystical experience.* Liguori, MO: Triumph Books.

Jaffe, A. (Ed.). (1989). *C. G. Jung: Memories, dreams, and reflections.* New York: Random House.

Jaworski, J. (1998). *Synchronicity: The inner path of leadership.* San Francisco: Berrett-Koehler.

Johnson, R. A. (1986). *Inner work: Using dreams and active imagination for personal growth.* San Francisco: HarperSanFrancisco.

Johnson, W. (1997). *Silent music: The science of meditation.* New York: Fordham University Press.

Jordan, J. (1999). *The musician's soul: A journey examining spirituality for performers, teachers, composers, conductors, and music educators.* Chicago: GIA Publications, Inc.

Jourdain, R. (1997). *Music, the brain, and ecstasy: How music captures our imagination.* New York: Avon Books.

Jung, C. G. (1960). *Collected works: Vol. 8. The structure and dynamics of the psyche.* New York: Princeton University Press.

Kabat-Zinn, J. (1994). *Wherever you go there you are: Mindfulness meditation in everyday life.* New York: Hyperion Books.

Karpay, E. (2000). *The everything total fitness book: A complete program to help you look—and feel—great.* Avon, MA: Adams Media Corporation.

Keating, T. (1997). *Open mind, open heart.* New York: The Continuum.

King, S. (1981). *Imagineering for health: Self-healing through the use of the mind.* Wheaton, IL: Quest Books.

Koestenbaum, P. (2002). *Leadership: The inner side of greatness—A philosophy for leaders.* San Francisco: Jossey-Bass.

Kraftsow, G. (1999). *Yoga for wellness: Healing with the timeless teachings of Viniyoga.* New York: Penguin.

Kundtz, D. (2000). *Everyday serenity: Meditations for people who do too much.* New York: MJF Books.

Lakein, A. (1973). *How to get control of your time and your life.* New York: Peter H. Wyden, Inc.

Lasater, J. (1995). *Relax and renew: Restful yoga for stressful times.* Berkeley, CA: Rodmell Press.

Levine, S. (1989). *A gradual awakening.* New York: Anchor Books.

Lewis, S. (Ed.). (2004, January/February). The music of relief. *Spirituality & Health, 7*(1), 18.

London, P. (1989). *No more secondhand art: Awakening the artist within.* Boston: Shambhala.

Lovric, M. (Ed.). (1993). *Friends: An illustrated treasury of friendship.* London: Royle Publications Ltd.

Luke, H. M. (2000). *Such stuff as dreams are made on: An autobiography and journals of Helen M. Luke.* New York: Parabola Books.

Malnar, K. A. (1996). *Personal and professional balance among female superintendents in Michigan's public schools.* Unpublished doctoral dissertation, Eastern Michigan University, Ypsilanti.

Malone, N. M. (2004, December). Reading with new eyes. *Sojourners, 33*(12), 8.

McAdams, R. P. (1998). Who'll run the schools? *American School Board Journal, 185*(8), 37–39.

McKay, J. (2004, Summer). Workaholism: Praised or the plague of school administrators? *AASA Journal of Scholarship and Practice, 1*(2), 6–9.

Merton, T. (1958). *Thoughts in solitude.* New York: Farrar, Straus & Giroux.

Metzger, C. (1997, January). Involuntary turnover of superintendents. *Thrust for Educational Leadership, 26*(4), 20–22, 44.

Metzger, C. (2003, November). Self/inner development of educational administrators: A national study of urban school district superintendents and college deans. *Urban Education, 38*(6), 665–687.

Metzger, C. (2004). *Self/inner development of educational administrators: Research and practice.* Unpublished manuscript, Office of Research and Sponsored Projects, California State University, Northridge.

Miller, W. (1979). *Dealing with stress: A challenge for educators.* Bloomington, IN: Phi Delta Kappa Educational Foundation.

Mitroff, I. I., & Denton, E. A. (1999). *A spiritual audit of corporate America.* San Francisco: Jossey-Bass.

Moore, T. (1992). *Care of the soul: A guide for cultivating depth and sacredness in everyday life.* New York: Harper Perennial.

Moore, T. (1994). *Soul mates: Honoring the mysteries of love and relationships.* New York: HarperCollins.

Morrissey, M. M. (1996). *Building your field of dreams.* New York: Bantam.

Murphy, B. (2002). *Zen and the art of knitting: Exploring the links between knitting, spirituality, and creativity.* Avon, MA: Adams Media.

Nelson, G. (2003, November 14). *Gifts my father never gave me.* Lecture presented at a meeting of the C. G. Jung Club of Orange County, Orange, CA.

Nelson, S. J. (2004). *Night wings: A soulful dreaming and writing practice.* Berwick, ME: Nicolas-Hays.

Nouwen, H. J. M. (1976). *Ich horte auf die Stille: Sieben Monate im Trappistenkloster* [I listened to the silence: Seven months in a Trappist monastery]. Freiburg, Germany: Herder. (Originally published as *Genessee diary: Report from a Trappist monastery.* Garden City, NY: Doubleday)

Orloff, J. (2004, May/June). Accessing sacred energy. *Spirituality & Health, 7*(3), 48–51.

Pinskey, R. (Trans.). (1994). *The inferno of Dante.* New York: Farrar, Straus and Giroux.

Progoff, I. (1992). *At a journal workshop: Writing to access the power of the unconscious and evoke creative ability.* New York: Penguin.

Pulley, M. L. (1997). *Losing your job—Reclaiming your soul.* San Francisco: Jossey-Bass.

Rilke, R. M. (1993). *Letters to a young poet*. New York: W. W. Norton.

Robinson, K. (2001). *Out of our minds: Learning to be creative*. Oxford, United Kingdom: Capstone.

Sanford, J. A. (1989). *Dreams: God's forgotten language*. San Francisco: HarperCollins.

Scott, R. O. (Ed.). (2002, Spring). Fifty ways to nourish your soul. *Spirituality & Health, 5*(1), 32–37.

Senge, P. M. (1990). *The fifth discipline: The art and practice of the learning organization*. New York: Doubleday.

Sergiovanni, T. J. (1992). *Moral leadership*. San Francisco: Jossey-Bass.

Stanley, J. (1999). *Reading to heal: How to use bibliotherapy to improve your life*. New York: Houghton Mifflin.

Susuki, S. (1996). *Zen mind, beginner's mind*. New York: Weatherhill.

Sweere, J. J. (2004). *Golden rules for vibrant health in body, mind, and spirit*. North Bergen, NJ: Basic Health Publications, Inc.

Thich Nhat Hanh. (1976). *The miracle of mindfulness: A manual on meditation*. Boston: Beacon Press.

Thich Nhat Hanh. (1987). *Being peace*. Berkeley, CA: Parallax Press.

Thompson, C. M. (2000). *The congruent life: Following the inward path to fulfilling work and inspired leadership*. San Francisco: Jossey-Bass.

Tolle, E. (1999). *The power of now*. Novato, CA: New World Library.

Van Dusen, W. (1999). *Beauty, wonder, and the mystical mind*. West Chester, PA: Chrysalis Books.

Versluis, A. (2004). *Awakening the contemplative spirit: Writing, gardening, and the inner life*. St. Paul, MN: New Grail Publishing.

Vouga, R. G. (2003, Fall). Why do effective administrators choose to remain in "the hot seat"? *Educational Leadership and Administration: California Professors of Educational Administration, 15*, 63–74.

Walsh, R. (1999). *Essential spirituality: The 7 central practices to awaken heart and mind*. New York: Wiley & Sons.

Wax, A. S., & Hales, L. W. (1990, April). *Can colleagues identify the burned out school administrator?* Paper presented at the annual meeting of the American Educational Research Association, Boston. (ERIC Document Reproduction Service No. ED 322 569)

Whitfield, C. L. (1993). *Boundaries and relationships: Knowing, protecting and enjoying the self*. Deerfield Beach, FL: Health Communications, Inc.

Whyte, D. (1996). *The heart aroused: Poetry and the preservation of the soul in corporate America*. New York: Doubleday.

Wolters, C. (Ed.). (1978). *The cloud of unknowing and other works*. New York: Penguin Classics.

Yehling, R. (2004, December). Mind of the body. *Science of Mind, 77*(12), 23–28.

Zukav, G. (1979). *The dancing Wu Li masters*. New York: William Morrow.

Index

**CORWIN
PRESS**

The Corwin Press logo—a raven striding across an open book—represents the union of courage and learning. Corwin Press is committed to improving education for all learners by publishing books and other professional development resources for those serving the field of PreK–12 education. By providing practical, hands-on materials, Corwin Press continues to carry out the promise of its motto: **"Helping Educators Do Their Work Better."**